CONTROLLING STRESS IN THE WORKPLACE

HOW YOU HANDLE WHAT HAPPENS

Controlling Stress in the Workplace

How You Handle What Happens

Rex P. Gatto, Ph.D.

Amsterdam • Johannesburg • London
San Diego • Sydney • Toronto

Editor: JoAnn Padgett
Page Compositor: Nicola Ruskin
Cover: John Odam Design Associates

Pfeiffer & Company
8517 Production Avenue
San Diego, California 92121-2280
(619) 578-5900 FAX (619) 578-2042

Library of Congress Cataloging in Publication Data
Gatto, Rex P.
Controlling stress in the workplace: how you handle what happens/Rex P. Gatto
p. cm.
Originally published: Pittsburgh: GTA Press, 1991.
Includes bibliographical references.
ISBN: 0-89384-218-4 (pbk.)
1. Job stress. 2. Stress management. I. Title
HF5548.85.G38 1993 92-51020
650'.01'9–dc20 CIP

Printed in the United States of America.
Printing 1 2 3 4 5 6 7 8 9 10

Dedication

When you work closely with an assistant every day, you may find that you lose sight of the friendship, support, and help that is given. I am fortunate to have a loyal and supporting friend as my assistant.

This book is dedicated to my assistant of many years, Carolyn Schenk.

Contents

Preface

It's all relative. No truer axiom has ever been uttered when explaining stress. What is "no big thing" to one person can be seen as a catastrophic event to someone else. Yet there is no way to escape stress—it is evident in every aspect of our lives. Although stress affects us at work and at home, it can be managed. By realizing and accepting stress as part of our existence, we can work to handle it and be productive in doing so. We must strive to make stress another part of the growth experience, not a barrier to happiness.

To deal with stress, we need to understand what it is and determine the causes of stress in our lives. For example, many drugs help you feel less anxious or stressed. Diazepam (Valium) is prescribed to many people in this country: "A conservative estimate indicates that at least 8,000 tons of Valium were consumed in the United States in 1977." (Tallman, et al. 1980). Yet Valium does not help you understand the symptoms and causes of stress. The pharmacological approach only deals with the results of anxiety (stress).

> "Throughout history, anxiety has been recognized as an inherent part of man's being. The definition of anxiety is as varied as the experience itself, and its biological basis is obscure. While anxiety may be thought of as an unpleasant

> state, characterized by uneasiness and apprehension, it is also a strong motivating force in many forms of behaviors and, like fear, has fundamental, adaptive, and perhaps evolutionary significance."
>
> *(Tallman, et al. 1980)*

Anxiety is an unpleasant emotional state or conflict, often caused by stress. Stress is part of our modern and changing lifestyles. The question is: "What do we do about the stress in our lives?" This is a difficult question to answer. Some stress may help you to accomplish a task on time; the same amount of stress may cause lack of sleep; and, depending on the individual, similar amounts of stress may cause physical harm.

First, let's examine what stress is. Stress usually comes from the "fight or flight" syndrome in which mental and physical demands come into conflict. These demands grow geometrically through work, family, and other relationships. Almost like a balloon filling with air, the stress continues to build until there is a feeling of being pushed to the limit. Generally, increasing control over a situation lessens the stress level in a situation and eases the pressure inside your balloon. This is why the copilot feels more stress than the pilot, assistants feel more stress than the boss, and vice presidents may feel more stress than the president; these subordinates are not in control of the situation.

When there is a lack of control and a high level of demands, stress can affect productivity. A lack of self-esteem and support from others should also be recognized and evaluated as causes of stress. In terms of the balloon analogy: What can we do to let air out of the balloon so that we don't feel so stretched?

Throughout this book we will discuss ways to relieve stress, such as opening lines of communication, establishing a realistic workload, making decisions, using humor, exercising, maintaining good nutrition, setting priorities and delegating, and using other relaxation techniques. These stress relievers will help to let some air out of your balloon. Addressing problem issues and creating possible solutions will lessen your stress and enhance the quality of your life.

Working through this book will help you to identify and diagnose causes of stress and begin to understand and deal with it. You'll complete exercises and develop a plan to lessen unwanted stress in your life. Use this book as an interactive self-counseling system. Work at your own pace and continually challenge yourself to implement the most appropriate method of stress reduction. You will be able to address your stress by asking yourself the right questions. And, most important, relax.

Instruction for Reflection

From this page on, you will practice ways to manage stress. The exercises throughout the book are designed to stimulate thoughts and feelings so that you can get a better grasp of what stress is and how it affects you. You may want to buy a notebook in which to write responses, or you can simply write in this book when responding to the inventory questions. If you buy a notebook, title it "Learning Log on Stress." Put your name and the date inside the front cover.

To get the most out of the exercises, challenge yourself by being introspective and honest. Contemplate and daydream about achieving what you want. It is important that you write your comments so that you can focus your thoughts and subsequently reread and reevaluate your ideas.

Periodically review your written responses and reflect on why you responded the way you did. Ask yourself, "Would I respond the same way now?" Learning to effectively deal with stress is a lifelong process of reflecting on how you manage everyday events.

1

Identifying Your Stress Level

Stress Inventories

In this chapter you will complete two inventories that will help you identify possible causes of your stress. The first inventory, "Are You Distressed?" will identify general stress; the second, "Work-Related Stressors," will identify specific elements of your work life that are stressful.

There are no right or wrong answers to the inventories. The only criteria are that you respond openly and honestly. The purpose of these inventories is to help you assess your level of stress and then to guide you in identifying general stressors in your life and in the workplace. The questions are based on a great deal of research that has been done in the area of stress. However, the real learning and management of stress will occur through the introspective feedback process. The term "feedback" should be thought of as a process by which you can express your thoughts about prior action in order to adapt to future action..."feed the future."

Take a deep, cleansing breath and begin the inventories with a positive outlook. You want to enhance your quality of life by lessening unwanted stress in the way you think and take action. Answer the following questions openly and honestly. Use this as a learning tool to identify what distresses you. Follow the same procedure for the "Work-Related Stressors" inventory.

Are You Distressed?

Instructions: Rate each answer 0 to 4 using the scale below and write a brief explanation in the space provided.

0 = Never; 1 = Rarely; 2 = Sometimes; 3 = Frequently; 4 = Often

Do you generally:

1. Get frustrated with minor problems? 0 1 2 3 4

   List the problems: ____________________

   ____

   ____

2. Avoid returning phone calls within a reasonable time frame? 0 1 2 3 4

   What particular call would you avoid? __

   ____

   ____

3. Avoid people or meetings, if possible? 0 1 2 3 4

   Whom or what would you like to avoid? _

   ____

   ____

4. "Run" yellow lights while driving? 0 1 2 3 4

   Explain: ____________________

   ____

   ____

5. Avoid giving full explanations to people? 0 1 2 3 4

   Explain: ____________________

   ____

   ____

0 = Never; 1 = Rarely; 2 = Sometimes; 3 = Frequently; 4 = Often

6. Watch the clock? 0 1 2 3 4

   *Why is time a concern?*_______________

7. Focus on completing work because of deadlines, rather than being concerned with the quality of your work? 0 1 2 3 4

   *Explain:*_______________

8. Avoid reviewing your material? 0 1 2 3 4

   List the problems: _______________

9. Delegate your work load knowing that quality will suffer? 0 1 2 3 4

   *Explain:*_______________

10. Leave meetings before you get what you want? 0 1 2 3 4

    *Explain:*_______________

0 = Never; 1 = Rarely; 2 = Sometimes; 3 = Frequently; 4 = Often

11. Feel that you are overloaded mentally and/or physically? 0 1 2 3 4

    Why? ___________________________

    ____

    ____

12. Hurry to complete projects without reassessing them? 0 1 2 3 4

    List any projects: ___________________________

    ____

    ____

13. Have an attitude of, "I'll get the job done, no matter what"? 0 1 2 3 4

    Why? ___________________________

    ____

    ____

14. Experience unusual behavior changes (become short tempered, quieter, or unmotivated)? 0 1 2 3 4

    List behavior changes: ___________________________

    ____

    ____

15. Skip lunch to get work done even when you are hungry? 0 1 2 3 4

    Why? ___________________________

    ____

    ____

0 = Never; 1 = Rarely; 2 = Sometimes; 3 = Frequently; 4 = Often

16. Avoid expressing your thoughts when something has upset you? 0 1 2 3 4

    What would you like to say? ___________

    ____

    ____

17. Feel frustrated by changes in the workplace (within the last eight months)? 0 1 2 3 4

    Identify any changes: ___________

    ____

    ____

18. Feel that your physical surroundings are dull, unattractive, and/or dreary? 0 1 2 3 4

    What could be improved? ___________

    ____

    ____

19. Feel concerned about your safety while working? 0 1 2 3 4

    Why? ___________

    ____

    ____

20. Feel that your job responsibilities are not challenging? 0 1 2 3 4

    Explain: ___________

    ____

    ____

0 = Never; 1 = Rarely; 2 = Sometimes; 3 = Frequently; 4 = Often

21. Feel that your work associates are not supportive? 0 1 2 3 4

*Explain:*______________________________

22. Feel frustrated by financial problems? 0 1 2 3 4

*Explain:*______________________________

23. Have conflicts with other employees? 0 1 2 3 4

*Explain:*______________________________

24. Feel frustrated with the organization's benefits package with regard to your family's needs? 0 1 2 3 4

*Explain:*______________________________

25. Feel of lack of trust in the workplace? 0 1 2 3 4

*Explain:*______________________________

0 = Never; 1 = Rarely; 2 = Sometimes; 3 = Frequently; 4 = Often

26. Feel that family problems are a constant source of pressure? 0 1 2 3 4
    Explain: ______________________________
    ____
    ____

27. Feel that conflicts among family members are a source of pressure? 0 1 2 3 4
    Explain: ______________________________
    ____
    ____

28. Have concerns about your physical well-being (within the past six months)? 0 1 2 3 4
    Explain: ______________________________
    ____
    ____

29. Feel that you have not clearly established work-related expectations (goals)? 0 1 2 3 4
    Explain: ______________________________
    ____
    ____

30. Feel you have not clearly accomplished personal expectations (goals)? 0 1 2 3 4
    Explain: ______________________________
    ____
    ____

Scoring: To total your number of stress points based on these questions, add the response rating (4, 3, 2, 1, or 0) for each question.

Total number of points______________

The total stress points indicate that the level of stress in your life is as follows:

120	to	90	points	=	Very stressful
89	to	60	points	=	Stressful
59	to	30	points	=	Not very stressful
29	to	0	points	=	Very little stress

Review your answers and explanations for each question. Are there any common causes (stressors) for your stress? Next you will identify additional causes of stress and develop solutions to lessen them.

Causes of Stress

As you identify the stressors in your life, think about which ones cannot be avoided and what changes you could make to lessen their impact. Possible catalysts for your stress might include work-related pressures, time management problems, and unrealistic workloads. In addition, self-conflict, resistance to change, refusal to challenge yourself, low self-esteem, lack of support from employees and/or family, and conflicts with others can cause great stress. Stress can also result from money problems, working in a hazardous environment, or not having a sense of accomplishment.

Analyze your responses to stressors. In this book or your notebook, write open and honest comments to yourself concerning your stressors and what you can realistically do to lessen stress in your life. Some ways to lessen stress include daily walks, aerobic exercise, a routine exercise schedule, quiet dinners, fifteen-minute periods reserved for daydreaming, low-stress hobbies, reading, and setting aside a daily block of time just for yourself. Remember, too, to give yourself credit for your accomplishments. Meditate, share your ideas and problems with someone, write a list of your stressors and possible solutions to lessen stress.

Identifying Stressors

On the following pages, write open, honest, and respectful comments to yourself. Trust your intuition. Review the "Are You Distressed?" inventory and group your thoughts under three categories: job, family, and self-related stressors. Then write an action plan to lessen your stress. Be very specific in your responses. Begin by analyzing all of the questions you rated as a 4.

1. Job-Related Stressors	Actions to Lessen Your Stressors
__________	__________
__________	__________
__________	__________
__________	__________
__________	__________
__________	__________
__________	__________
__________	__________

2. Family-Related Stressors	Actions to Lessen Your Stressors
__________	__________
__________	__________
__________	__________
__________	__________
__________	__________
__________	__________
__________	__________
__________	__________

3. Self-Induced Stressors (internal conflict)	Actions to Lessen Your Stressors
______________________	______________________
______________________	______________________
______________________	______________________
______________________	______________________
______________________	______________________
______________________	______________________
______________________	______________________
______________________	______________________

Summary Comments:

____

____

____

____

You may want to take a ten-minute break before you begin the next inventory, "Work-Related Stressors."

Work-Related Stressors

Instructions: Answer the following questions openly and honestly to identify stressors at work. Rate each answer 0, 1, or 2 using the scale below.

0 = Rarely (if ever); 1 = Sometimes; 2 = Usually

1. Are you a decision maker?	0 1 2
2. Do you continually have to monitor people (performance appraisals), information, or equipment?	0 1 2
3. Does your job require complex physical or mental activities?	0 1 2
4. Is communication a major factor in each of your job responsibilities?	0 1 2
5. Is your work environment filled with anxiety?	0 1 2
6. Do you work in a hazardous environment?	0 1 2
7. Do you work in an unstructured environment (not knowing what could occur day to day)?	0 1 2
8. Does your work environment change continually (people, equipment, type of work)?	0 1 2
9. Is there conflict between your family's needs and your work priorities?	0 1 2
10. Are your job responsibilities unclear (you don't know what should be done next)?	0 1 2

0 = Rarely (if ever); 1 = Sometimes; 2 = Usually

11. Do you feel you lack support from your supervisor/manager or other employees? 0 1 2

12. Do you feel you lack support from your family? 0 1 2

13. Do you lack involvement in the decision-making process? 0 1 2

14. Do you lack the self-confidence to perform up to your own standards when you do not know the possible outcome of the given project? 0 1 2

15. Do you lack the self-esteem to speak up when you disagree with work-related issues? 0 1 2

16. Do you feel that you are doing too much at work and at home? 0 1 2

17. Are you concerned about and aware of the continually changing environment at work? 0 1 2

18. Do you lack clearly defined career expectations (goals)? 0 1 2

19. Do you lack the finances and benefits needed to fulfill your family's needs? 0 1 2

20. Do you have a feeling that you are not accomplishing what you could, given the opportunity? 0 1 2

Scoring: To total your work-related stress points based on these questions, add the response rating (2, 1, or 0) for each question.

Total number of points ____________

The total stress points indicate that your level of stress in the workplace is as follows:

40	to	30	points	=	Very stressful
29	to	20	points	=	Stressful
19	to	10	points	=	Not very stressful
9	to	0	points	=	Very little stress

Your survival in the workplace depends not on what happens to you, but rather on how you handle what happens. Research (Baron, 1986; Shaw and Riskind, 1983) indicates that work-related stressors include the following, listed in random order:

- Communication
- Decision making
- People monitoring (supervising/managing)
- Complex, manual dexterity tasks
- Hazardous or unsafe work environment
- Uncertainty about job responsibilities or what needs to be accomplished
- Interruptions, such as phone calls
- Changes in the job, department, organization
- Lack of support, involvement, or self-esteem
- Conflict between work and family
- Different working, learning, and personality styles among coworkers

Review your responses on the "Work-Related Stressors" inventory and contemplate any action you feel necessary to create change. Begin by listing the work-related stressors that you rated highest (as 2s) and comment on how you might be able to lessen them.

Work-Related Stressors	Actions to Lessen Your Stressors
______________________	______________________
______________________	______________________
______________________	______________________
______________________	______________________
______________________	______________________
______________________	______________________
______________________	______________________
______________________	______________________
______________________	______________________
______________________	______________________
______________________	______________________
______________________	______________________
______________________	______________________
______________________	______________________

The following are ways in which stress relates to your frame of mind (Baron, 1986):

- Stress induces mood shifts and emotions.
- Job-related stress can lower self-esteem.
- Job-related stress relates to job satisfaction.

Inventory Summary

After completing both inventories, review your responses. Now reflect on how to control stress in your work life. What choices must you make to help you lessen stress in your life? Are there obstacles preventing you from achieving what you want? If so, identify those obstacles (people, events, situations, accomplishments) and write exactly what you feel about them. Write until you feel you have exhausted all possibilities. Summarize your responses from both inventories. Write an agenda for action.

Model for Developing an Action Plan

1. Identify what you want to accomplish. What results do you anticipate from lessening your stress levels?

   ____

   ____

   ____

   ____

   ____

   ____

2. Examine your responses. What is preventing you from achieving what you want?

   ____

   ____

   ____

   ____

   ____

   ____

3. Develop your action plan based on your responses to Questions 1 and 2.

____

____

____

____

____

____

Reflection Model

Utilizing the following reflection model will help you become aware of where you are and where you want to go (mentally, physically, and philosophically) given your wants, needs, desires, and motivations.

Develop a plan to act. This is essential when dealing with stress. Be proactive. Initiate action rather than being reactive or passive. Plan to achieve your potential continually by lessening the unwanted stress in your life.

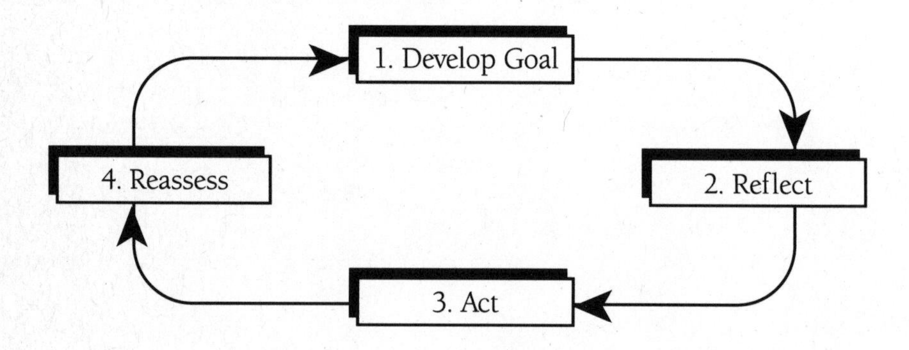

1. Develop Goal–The first step in determining how you'll tackle a stressful element of your life is to develop a goal. Any analysis requires collecting data about yourself and assembling it for review. Based on the inventories, collect data relevant to what's causing your stress and determine what you can do about these stressors. Develop a realistic plan of action based on your data.
2. Reflect–Now is the time to brainstorm ideas to deal with your stressors. Don't limit yourself. Create strategies and explore methods for implementing your ideas.
3. Act–Implement your ideas for a strategy/methodology within a specific, realistic time frame. Be patient and maintain momentum once you begin to combat the stressors you've identified.

4. Reassess—Because no process is 100 percent foolproof, you'll want to assess your progress periodically. This review actually occurs at each step in the process.
   a. Recognize strengths and problems. (Utilize your strengths.)
   b. Assess risks.
   c. Collect unbiased information.
   d. Have the courage to continue.

Write your comments below.

Develop Goal:

____

____

____

Reflect:

____

____

____

Act:

____

____

____

Reassess:

____

____

____

Analyzing Work-Related Stressors

The same approach to handling stress day after day or year after year may not be productive for you or the people with whom you interact. People naturally change because of societal pressure, the job market, and new interests. The best way to "go with the flow" is to assess where you are and where you want to be, then adapt and react.

Each of us faces doors that we need to open. Writing an action plan will help you to shape a key to open current and future doors. View your action plan as a tool to focus your thoughts and energies so you can initiate action. Create a plan of action that focuses on healthy and helpful methods of dealing with stress.

Stop and reflect on how you can successfully lessen stress through measurable actions (methods). Set a time frame for implementing these actions, then assess your accomplishments.

Review your notes. Remember that life offers many possibilities. What do you want?

Based on your answers to the preceding questions about work, these pages will help to focus your thoughts and will let you identify and examine stressors in your life. Let's specifically address the work-related stressors.

Reflect on how you can effectively deal with your causes of stress. Review each response to the twenty questions in the "Work-Related Stressors" inventory and write explanations for your answers.

1. ____

____

____

____

2. ______________________________

____

____

____

3. ______________________________

____

____

____

4. ______________________________

____

____

____

5. ______________________________

____

____

____

6. ______________________________

____

____

____

7. ______________________________

____

____

____

8. ____

____

____

____

9. ____

____

____

____

10. ____

____

____

____

11. ____

____

____

____

12. ____

____

____

____

13. ____

____

____

____

14. ____

15. ____

16. ____

17. ____

18. ____

19. ____

20. ____

After you have written your thoughts, read and analyze your responses. Underline and/or circle key words or issues that you feel will help you to focus on actions to lessen stress.

Take time now to page through Chapter 1. Review what you have written. Review this chapter periodically to measure changes and accomplishments and to assess your ability to control and lessen stress.

2

Organizing to Overcome Stress

Thought Provokers

Take a few moments to read through the following thoughts about stress.

- The presence of stress is universal, but the causes of stress differ.
- You can lessen your stress and learn how to relax.
- Survival depends not so much on what happens but on how you handle what happens.
- Life is not a catastrophe; it is a great event waiting to unfold. Give yourself credit for what you do. Utilize your potential and all available resources.
- Accept where you are today and plan for the future. Do not dwell on, "I should have..."
- You seldom meet someone else's expectations—you can only meet your own. Great stress can result from trying to be someone you are not.
- Search for the causes and reasons for your success and your happiness.
- Self-induced stress may be the result of not appropriately applying your work style to your job responsibilities.
- Something that is stressful for you (speaking to a group, writing reports, attending business meetings) may be a source of relaxation for others.
- By changing your attitude, you can change your job and lessen job-related stress without changing your job description.

Develop a contract with yourself as a challenge to lessen stress in your life. Examine your strengths and others' strengths in particular areas. Why is it that you and others are successful?

A Developmental Contract

What do you want to accomplish by reading and completing this book?

____

____

____

How will your strengths help you?

____

____

____

What is your commitment to yourself regarding stress?

____

____

____

Who is responsible for accomplishing what you want?

____

____

____

What obstacles must you overcome?

____

____

____

A Brief History of Stress

Before you can lessen stress in your life, you must identify the causes of stress (or stressors). You have already begun this process by completing the preceding two inventories. The objective is not to eradicate stress, but to effectively identify, address, and control your stressors. The challenge of life is to maintain a balance of needs, desires, and external pressures (money, time), while achieving your potential.

Our response to stress seems to have originated in prehistoric man's fight-or-flight reactions to frightening situations. Today, we usually do not fight or leave; we have been socialized to maintain the status quo. Often this contradicts our natural instincts and causes stress.

Stress is an emotional and physiological response. We react mentally, emotionally, and physically, which causes the muscle structures within our body to react. The body—mentally and physically—continually reacts to stimuli. If the response creates bodily and mental tension via the psyche, then some type of stress will emerge.

Stress is a human function. It is the body's way of dealing with difficult or unfamiliar situations. If you reflect on and assess the situation without being overly critical, you can learn how to deal with stressful situations in ways that are acceptable to yourself and others.

Defining Stressors

Although the presence of stress is universal, the causes of stress may vary from person to person. Something that is stressful for one person may be a source of relaxation for another. You should identify what causes you stress and whether that stress is helpful *(eustress)* or harmful *(distress)*.

Eustress: good stress; an uplifting feeling or anxiousness.

Distress: a persistent condition that negatively affects you physically (rapid breathing and pulse, high blood pressure), mentally (anxiety, tension), and behaviorally (short tempered, irrational). Characterized by heavy workload; not being able to complete a job to your satisfaction; performing tasks you do not like; and time constraints.

Stress anxiety precludes learning and can alter your behavior or ability to perform. If you are tense or anxious before a special event, you will demonstrate that in your actions. Once you are aware of a cause of stress, you will be able to respond positively. In other words, if when you give a presentation you get nervous, you can develop a strategy of presentation designed to deal with the cause of your stress. The more you are aware of your causes of stress, the more you can utilize your acquired knowledge (analysis of your stress) in that given situation.

(Kaplan, H., Sadock, B., 1980)

What Is Stress and What Are Stressors?

Stressors are major changes in a person's ongoing life pattern. Stress is a complex mediation process that occurs between the life event and the biological responses of the body. This mediation process involves a cognitive interpretation of the event in light of past history and experiences, an emotional reaction, and an attempt at coping.

1. Stress is nonspecific, although each stressor has both specific effects (sweating) and nonspecific effects (development of ulcers, rapid heart rate, queasy stomach).
2. A stressor is whatever produces nonspecific effects (e.g., public speaking, family discord).
3. Psychological events can produce the same stress response as physical stressors.

4. Some stressors produce good stress, or eustress, and others produce bad stress, or distress.
5. Stress is always a matter of degree; it varies with the person, situation, and environment.
6. Stress in humans can be moderated by various treatments and techniques.

(Selye, 1980)

In the fifteenth century stress meant pressure or physical strain; the seventeenth century described it as hardship or adversity; twentieth century stress was considered as psychosomatic medicine and a cause for ill health or mental disease. In the 1930's the word *stressor* was used to describe an external cause or stimulus for stress and the state of bodily disequilibrium as *stress*.

Events that act as stressors generally relate to status, power, territory, values, and beliefs. The bodily reactions to stressors are basically attempts at adaptation, and if the stressors are not too extreme or too chronic, such attempts to adapt are usually successful.

(Kaplan, H., Sadock, B., 1985)

For example, a short-term stressor such as a high-energy sensation when you must make a presentation can be beneficial; however, a daily, persistent stressor such as deadlines may not allow the body to adapt successfully and physical problems such as stomach ulcers may occur.

Stress, like motivation, cannot be observed directly. Rather, it is inferred or indirectly observed. Stress is measured by identifying stressors (as you did in the inventory) and by measuring bodily changes. Whereas motivation is measured by the effort exerted to accomplish something, stress can be measured by physical symptoms or by the failure to realize your potential because of the effects of stress.

External and Internal Work Stressors

The results of stressors within the workplace can produce a work stress syndrome, tiredness, irritability or job dissatisfaction, inability to concentrate, and burnout. These stressors may be internal or external.

External: policies and procedures, inappropriate or poor working relationships, repetitive or physically demanding job.

Internal: unrealistic expectations, personal needs are not met (unsatisfactory compensation), lack of recognition, lack of self-respect, and indecisiveness.

Some common results of this stress are boredom, apathy, and a negative attitude toward management, coworkers, customers, the organization, and self.

(Kaplan, H., Sadock, B., 1985)

Keep in mind that stress is a neurological function. A way to deal with stress is to understand what stimulates the brain to experience stress. For example, our "fight or flight" syndrome is a biological function that evolved from the cave man. Today, however, we often cannot "fight" or "flee" our situations. Rather, we must remain in the situation without addressing the cause of stress. However, conflict and arguing are the modern-day equivalents of fighting, while denial equates to flight. Thus, to handle stress effectively, you must accept that something is causing you to react this way. But this is a difficult realization, and taking action may create more stress.

Reactions to Stress

A major cause of stress comes from restraining the expressive release of stressors, which then continue to build and manifest themselves, thereby causing more stress. It's important to express the unexpressed. Psychologists suggest that you find ways to release stressors. For example, suppose you are feeling hostility toward or guilt about someone who has died. Psychologists would recommend that you write a letter to the deceased person, expressing your hostility or guilt, as a way to vent your feelings. It is healthy to express what you feel and, often, writing allows you to express what you may not want to say to someone in person.

The typical reaction to stress is self-denial—holding in your feelings, avoiding the situation.

Denial: the refusal to accept life experience; a way in which people deal with a painful experience (e.g., breakup of a marriage or relationship). Examples: continual/habitual lack of assuming job responsibilities or requirements; constant tardiness (denial of time); drug or alcohol abuse.

Denial is a type of "flight" from a difficult situation without really addressing the issue. People practice denial because it permits them to escape the reality of the situation. Denial creates a false belief that replaces the unpleasant reality. It is important for each of us to confront ourselves and the issues in our lives through self-reflection. Concepts of reality should not be denied. Instead, address these concepts and understand them in relationship to the "big picture" of your life.

Express your thoughts—write whatever you feel. Confront yourself. Mentally discuss and address your internal conflicts. Write them down.

Stressful Events and Experiences of Stress

A list of the catalysts for the most stressful events in our lives has been compiled by Holmes and Rahe (1967). Following is an adaptation of their research.

- Death of a spouse
- Divorce
- Separation
- Death of a family member
- Major personal injury or illness
- Marriage
- Being fired from a job
- Retirement
- Death of a close friend
- Financial problems
- Problems interacting with in-laws or a boss
- Dealing with change

Plotting Your Response to Stressful Events

Remember, stress is not caused by these events alone. How we choose to interpret and give meaning to these life events creates individual stressors. Stress is always with us; it manifests itself at different stages and levels as we move through life. With this in mind, review the accompanying Stress Continuum.

Plot your stress level on the continuum after you have evaluated four points: environment/events, people and interactions, self-interpretation, and drugs and other chemicals. What causes you great stress? Plot that on the top half of the continuum. Lesser stressors should be plotted on the lower half of the continuum.

Stress Continuum

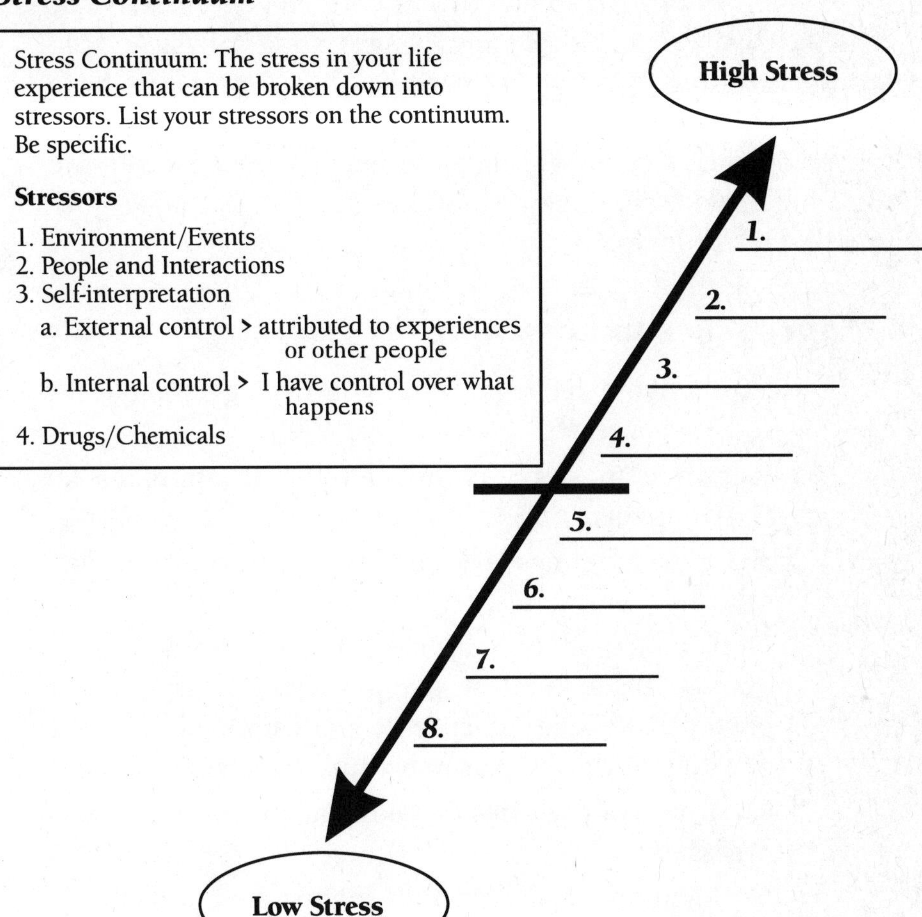

Use this exercise to determine the level of stress in your life based on the stressors you have identified in your life. Use this continuum as a way to identify your stress level and to establish priorities in dealing with stress.

Outcomes of Stressors

Though many of life's problems are minor, stress can be fatal. For this reason, stress must be identified (expressed) and methodically reduced. Following are some physical reactions resulting from stress: increased blood pressure, heart rate, and respiration; muscle constriction commonly in the neck or back; headaches; ulcers; stomach problems; nervous stomach; general anxiety; emotional responses (anger, fear, guilt, lack of love).

Approaches to Lessening Stressors

1. Express your feelings. Write your thoughts about the causes of stress.
2. Identify your stressors and develop an approach for lessening them.
3. Share your feelings with someone with whom you feel safe and comfortable.
4. Find a method of relieving stress. Examples: walk, exercise, listen to music, attend social gatherings (companionship), read, practice deep breathing. (Be careful of eating or drinking as a method of relaxing.)
5. Confront your worries by taking action and not avoiding issues.
6. Try to eliminate alcohol and caffeine in your diet.
7. Establish attainable goals toward which you can direct your energy.
8. Take personal responsibility for the quality of your life.

3

Controlling Stress

The following is a case study about an employee named Bill. As you read about Bill, think about the stress-related concepts that you have read about, assessed, and reflected upon. The case study is a way for you to learn how to lessen stress through the example of another person. Look for causes of stress in Bill's life. What would you would say to Bill if he were a friend of yours? If you were objectively counseling Bill, what would you advise him to do? Use this case study to refine and focus your thoughts about stress.

The technique of writing your feelings is used and explained in greater detail following the case study. For now, practice the technique of writing unexpressed thoughts in your own way.

Case Study

Bill is in his mid-forties. He is a middle manager in the manufacturing division of a large chemical corporation. Everyone in the office seems to get along with him. Bill knows the twenty employees he manages, their spouses, and most of their children. On Mondays he talks about sports and other recreation, and he generally manages to create a pleasant atmosphere in the office. By all outward appearances, Bill is cool, calm, and relaxed.

Bill was promoted five years ago from the research and development department to the manufacturing division. His main responsibilities are to understand the needs of the customer and to be aware of what the competition is developing. Then he updates senior executives as to market and competitive trends. He is the middle man between the customer and the corporation. He continually feels that he is fighting the clock. Bill realizes he tries to do too much, but he thinks, "I'll try to do it anyway."

Almost every morning he rushes to work early to get a jump on completing his work. Sometimes on his way to work he "runs" yellow lights because he is anxious to get to the job. It seems as though he is always "fighting fires" and managing crises. Last week a worker was injured by spilled chemicals, and Bill had to call the employee's wife and file all of the necessary medical forms. He then had to explain to the group vice president why his group's safety record is so bad. He simply said, "We are under a lot of pressure to produce."

Phone calls continually interrupt Bill's workday, and he is always in meetings. Often it takes him half a day just to return phone calls and even longer to actually reach the person whose call he is returning. He leaves so many voice mail messages that he forgets who and why he called. Bill wants to delegate more responsibilities to others, but he thinks that he can do the work more efficiently. He knows better than anyone what the executives and the customers want and need.

Bill is getting to work earlier and leaving later to try to get the job done. Bill knows he should exercise, but he doesn't have time. It seems that he goes to work and lives on coffee and cigarettes; however, he usually manages to have lunch.

Bill's two sons play on high school sports teams, and he often misses their games because he is at work or is traveling. His wife understands that he is under a lot of pressure but still would like him to be at home more. Bill feels caught between two worlds—neither of which are going well.

Bill likes his job and receives a fair salary, but the demands on him are consuming his life. He lives in an affluent neighborhood with an excellent school system. Both of the boys will be in college in less than four years. To quit his job and find another one with less pressure is out of the question. "Who would take a scientist in his mid-forties with an MBA and pay the same salary?"

Sometimes Bill's back feels tied up in knots. Last week, Bill felt a tightness in his chest while in a meeting. He started to become warm and perspire. He thought, "I have to relax. I'll be all right. I just have to take deep breaths and lay off the cigarettes."

Bill knows he will only have to do this a few more years until the division gets on its feet and meets all the quotas. Bill says, "I can handle it." Sometimes Bill wishes he could forget the entire job and go fishing.

Case Study Exercise

What advice would you give to Bill? Begin by discussing the following issues.

Ways to lessen Bill's job-related distress:

____

____

____

____

Bill's health needs:

____

____

____

____

Bill's family needs:

____

____

____

____

Self-denial:

____

____

____

____

Time management:

____

____

____

____

Leadership (people vs. task orientation):

____

____

____

____

Management style:

____

____

____

____

Writing Techniques to Lessen Stress

What are some techniques that Bill could use to express his thoughts? It is not enough to ponder or contemplate an action plan. Distressful thoughts should be put on paper and analyzed. Written words can be analyzed and interpreted differently than spoken words. Writing your ideas is not a panacea, but it is an objective way to record, analyze, and reflect on your stressful thoughts.

If you are frustrated or anxious about a situation (work, family, and/or self), try writing a letter to yourself describing what you are feeling about the situation. Write until there is nothing that you have not said. Don't hold back; express the emotions you feel. Look at the following examples.

Exercise 1

1. Express all of your thoughts on paper. Use statements beginning with "I am fed up with..." or "I can't stand it when...'"

   Expressing the unexpressed as to why you are "fed up" or "can't stand" something will let you focus directly on the issues. Instead of thinking and reflecting and letting yourself mentally churn, you can identify the specific problems. The following example illustrates how one person might have written these comments.

   > I am fed up with John who continually tells me what should be done. He thinks he knows what should be done and always has an answer. This really makes me angry. I just can't listen any more. He always has an answer. He knows what he knows, but...he doesn't know what I know—he always has something to say...

2. Put this paper away for a few hours or a day.

3. Reread the paper expressing your thoughts. Go back through the text and underline points of stress or key statements. Analyze what you wrote and why you felt the way you did.
4. Develop a realistic action plan to deal with the situation.

   An action plan might be as follows:

   a. Speak with John and let him know my ideas.

   b. Talk with another employee or friend.

   c. Walk to relieve daily tension.

Exercise 2

Try this approach if you are frustrated or anxious about a statement or with something that you regret saying. Take a piece of paper and divide it into three equal columns. Label the columns "Statements," "Causes," and "Outcomes" and fill in each column as noted.

Statement	Causes	Outcomes
	What caused this to happen?	Express the worst and best outcomes.

Analyze your response to the three columns and develop a plan of action. Do not let your ego stand in the way of resolution, but do not deny your personal needs.

Example A

Statement	Causes	Outcomes
Said I would never work with her!	I was angry about the meeting with Mary this morning.	She is really upset with me; we will have a difficult time working together (worst); I will talk to Mary; we will discuss it and improve our working relationship (best).

Action Plan

See Mary and explain that I did not mean to say…

Example B

Statement	Causes	Outcomes
I can't stand the pressure frm the deadlines. My neck tightens, my stomach churns. This is affecting my life!	Work, work, work!	This is taking its toll on my effectiveness at work. I am short-tempered! This is going to continue until I quit (worst); I am going to talk with my boss to make positive changes (best).

Action Plan

Speak with my boss; develop a better "to do" and "I did" list; schedule; delegate more; walk at lunch; take 10 minutes in the middle of the day to relax; give myself credit for what I am doing well; stop accepting unrealistic deadlines; realize that I can only produce a specific quantity of work; be assertive in expressing my viewpoints of realistic time demands with my boss.

Choosing and Using the Exercises

Use one of these techniques and express stressors/frustrations in your life. Write until you have nothing left to say. Next, reflect on what you have written. How do you feel? If you are still angry, express why. Underline key words that indicate causes of stress. Develop a plan of action to control and lessen your stress. Don't practice denial like Bill in the case study.

Overcoming Distress

Eustress and distress are part of the human condition. Identify the causes of distress in your life and develop a plan to change the distressful situation(s). Follow these six basic steps for handling stress.

1. Identify what distresses you. Using the first writing technique, list the problems (job, family, person, habits, etc.) that create distress for you. Put the paper away for a few hours or for a day, then read it again.
2. After the second reading, examine the distressful situations and write possible solutions for lessening the distress. Removing yourself from a particular environment is one solution. However, there are probably several other solutions to lessen the distress of job responsibilities.
3. Discuss the things that create stress for you with people who are presently experiencing the same distressful problems, or with a spouse or friend who has experienced the same type of situation. Just knowing that someone else has (or had) the same problem(s) or is sympathetic can be a source of relief.
4. Honor your reasons for being distressed and plan ways to address the causes. Create a strategy for dealing with daily work-related distress. Distress will not go away just because you ignore it. Accept what you wrote and create a strategy for change.
5. Prioritize your strategy for alleviating distress. Writing your thoughts and feelings may, in itself, lessen your anxiety in stressful situations. Establish an organized plan of action to deal with what stresses you.
6. Establish a routine at the end of the day to help you unwind (listen to the radio, watch television, walk, do deep breathing, read, exercise). Give yourself some

individual attention to dissipate the level of anxiety/frustration (stress). Dissipating the level of stress is called Tension Discharge Rate (TDR) (Matteson Ivancevich, 1983).

Write responses to these statements in your notebook.

1. In general, I become distressed when

____

____

____

____

____

____

____

____

____

2. I could lessen my feelings of distress by

____

____

____

____

____

____

____

____

____

3. In general, I feel my best when

____

____

____

____

____

____

____

____

____

Analyze what you have written. Make sure to continually implement the positive actions you identify to feel your best.

3 C's for Lessening Stress

How you handle stressful situations greatly depends on how you interpret or give meaning to three concepts: Commitment, Control, and Challenge. These three C's determine whether situations are stressful, relaxing, intense, happy, and so on.

1. Commitment

What are you willing to do to be satisfied? For what values are you willing to fight? What is the purpose and meaning of what you want to accomplish? This is the difference between fighting for a principle or forgetting or avoiding it. Maslow (1970) called these "Being Values." Commitment brings culture, intellect, desire, opportunity, and achievement together. Maslow discussed values in terms of beauty, perfection, truth, and justice. What do these four words mean in your life?

2. Control

Do you have a sense of control over your future? Are you an influencer or a decision maker in your life's work and direction? Have you accepted yourself and given yourself due credit?

Strive to find meaning in your life. As Frankl says in his book, *Man's Search for Meaning*, "...turn suffering into human achievement; derive from guilt the opportunity to change oneself for better; derive from life's changes an incentive to take responsible action; happiness should not be pursued but should ensure." What will cause you to live an enhanced quality of life?

You can also control some of your stress through diet. Smoking cigarettes and drinking alcohol and or a lot of coffee does not help you control your physical stress. Be careful of consuming a lot of sugar, processed foods, and high cholesterol foods. Eating fresh fruits and vegetables within a balanced diet and, not overeating, can help your stress level.

3. *Challenge*

Do you challenge yourself to reach your potential? Do you perceive change as a challenge or as a loss of safety and security—a threat? Maslow (1970) stated that people should continually be trying to self-actualize on individual terms. In other words, you should try to fulfill your capacity to become human. Do not apply old concepts to present situations. Instead, deal with the present according to the situation, desire, opportunity, and your own skill.

Stress Within Your Corporate Culture

Take time to reflect how you perceive the business climate that surrounds you (daily requirements, long-standing rules and regulations, work pressures). What is customary and accepted within your business environment? What individual behavior is rewarded or rejected? Which of your strengths (assertiveness, interpersonal skills, writing abilities) are accepted or rejected within your corporate culture?

On the Corporate Culture Diagram (see page 54), write a strength or weakness next to "You" in each of the four quadrants. Then write down the strengths and weaknesses for your "Supervisor" and for "Other Employees" (with whom you interact frequently) in the appropriate "acceptance" or "rejection" quadrant. List what you perceive to be common strengths, weaknesses, acceptances, and rejections shared by you, your supervisor, and other employees.

Draw the diagram in your notebook. You can substitute other descriptors as you feel appropriate. For example, substitute spouse for employee, or teacher for supervisor, then respond to the relationship and climate.

Write your strengths. Are they accepted or rejected by your supervisor?

Example: Strength—I talk a lot; it is a strength with some employees and customers, but is rejected by my supervisor. Weakness—I am late turning in paperwork. My boss rejects it; she gets angry. Other employees think I am okay for aggravating the boss.

Corporate Culture Diagram

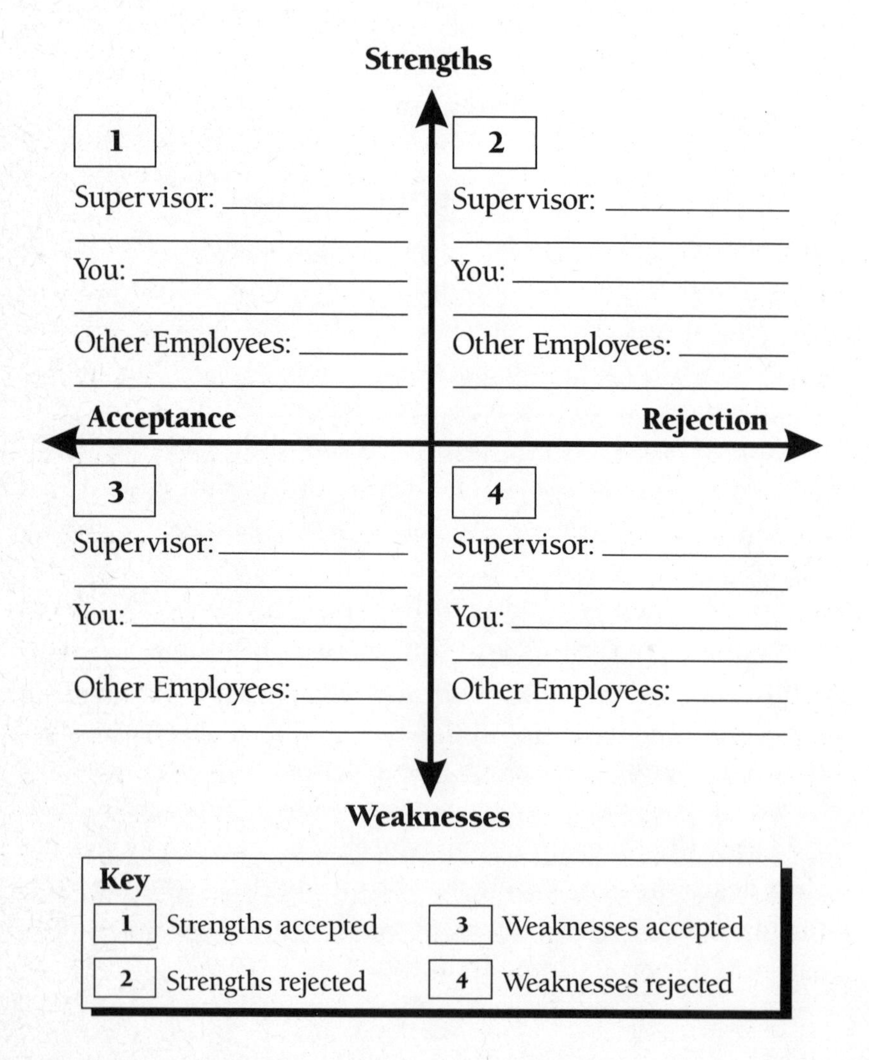

Examine the acceptance and rejection sides of the quadrant. Reflecting on your perceptions of what personal strengths and weaknesses are rejected or accepted may indicate what causes stress for you within your work environment.

Change, often the leading cause of anxiety, stress, and conflicts, does not usually occur suddenly within a corporate culture. It develops gradually. Pressures and anxieties are like boiling water in a tea kettle. You put cool water in the kettle, and over a period of time changes in the water occur because of catalysts (stove, a heating element, fire, etc.). Because you introduce change factors (heat), the water that was once cool begins to boil.

Corporate cultures change as do the physical properties of water brought to a boil. Changes over time can and do affect employees physically, mentally, and behaviorally. The corporate culture, like stress or any other life function, has no meaning until you individually interpret and conceptually identify your relationship within that environment. Continual reflection about the work environment will make you aware of and sensitive to your perceptions and actions.

When the kettle of boiling water is removed from the source of heat (the catalyst), the water will eventually return to a cooler state, but it will never be as it was prior to boiling (i.e., water is lost due to steam). So, too, when the catalysts for anxiety, stress, and conflicts are eliminated from the corporate environment, the corporate culture never returns to its prior state—this is neither good nor bad. This is the dynamic state of interaction that we may experience and interpret as distressful situations, occasions of eustress, or periods of calm.

In summary, all environments change—some more rapidly than others. Your ability to adapt or creatively develop alternatives (problem solving) determines how well you will be able to handle the situations found in your particular corporate culture.

Interactive Exercise

1. Based on the Corporate Culture Diagram, discuss with someone (friend, colleague, spouse) the causes of stress in your workplace. These stressors do not have to be specific to you. Discuss any and all stressors that you feel are present in your workplace. This is a method of relaxing in a safe environment while verbally expressing your thoughts.
2. Discuss possible solutions to the identified stressors.
3. Write a list of all the stressors that were identified. Remember, you are not the only one with stress. Sometimes we feel alone, but all of us have stressors.

Stressor	Solution
1.____________________	1.____________________
____________________	____________________
2.____________________	2.____________________
____________________	____________________
3.____________________	3.____________________
____________________	____________________
4.____________________	4.____________________
____________________	____________________
5.____________________	5.____________________
____________________	____________________
6.____________________	6.____________________
____________________	____________________

Relaxation Techniques

To help alleviate stress you must first identify causes and then take action. Another approach is to create an environment in which you can create relaxation and calm. There are many ways to deal with stress; here are a few.

Deep Breathing

Take your pulse. Beats per minute = ___ before relaxation and ___ after relaxation.

To measure your relaxation, you may want to use a Biodot (a small device that tells whether your hand is too cool, which suggests uneven temperatures in your body possibly caused by stress). Place the Biodot on the skin between your index finger and thumb on the back of your hand. Sit in a comfortable and relaxed position. Now you are ready to practice the breathing relaxation exercise.

Color Indicator of Biodot

Color		Indicator
Amber	=	Tense
Yellow	=	Unsettled
Green	=	Involved (normal)
Turquoise	=	Relaxed
Blue	=	Calm
Violet	=	Very relaxed

Breathing Exercise for Relaxing

1. Sit in a relaxed position.
2. Play slow, soft, symphonic music (second movement of a classical symphony).
3. Regulate your breathing (stomach breathing; do not move your chest).
4. Breathe in on 4 slow counts.

5. Hold your breath for 4 slow counts.
6. Exhale on 4 slow counts.
7. Hold your breath for 4 slow counts.
8. Think peaceful thoughts. Picture yourself at the beach, listen to the sound of the waves, feel the warm sun on your face.
9. Continue this cycle for approximately 5 minutes.
10. Check your pulse (and Biodot, if used).

Another Relaxation Technique

Rub your hands and wrists under very warm water to produce a relaxed feeling. This may be useful if you are anxious about giving a presentation and your hands are cold or trembling. The warm water will relax and comfort you. Try it!

A Favorite Technique: Daydreaming

A useful way to decrease anxiety or stress is to daydream. Daydreaming, one of the oldest and most effective methods for stress reduction, provides an instant escape from the day-to-day trials of living. Think about close friends, fun vacations, good food, or anything that makes you happy.

Set aside approximately fifteen minutes of undisturbed time. Sit comfortably so that there is no muscle tension. Put your hands on your stomach to ensure that you breathe deeply. Close your eyes. Picture the beach with waves gently lapping along the shore. Breathe deeply. Feel the warm sun on your face; hear the surf breaking on the shore. Concentrate on breathing deeply (two breaths in every five-second period) and focus. Take your time; relax. Slowly come back to your environment after ten to fifteen minutes.

4

Identifying Your Stress Management Style

Managing Stress

A common type of stressor involves the interactive relationships among people. Some people are domineering; others lack maturity; some are not focused on what they want to accomplish; and still others react only to external forces rather than to internal conviction. Interacting with people who exhibit these behavioral styles can be a source of stress. In a given situation, everyone, to some degree, can fall into the aforementioned descriptors. Some people are going to be less able to interact harmoniously than others. Behavioral styles, however, are learned and can be modified or unlearned.

Because work is demanding, you may be in continual conflict with yourself (setting unrealistic expectations) and with other employees. This can be extremely stressful, but there are solutions to relieve your stress. Try adapting some of your working characteristics so that you interact with employees more effectively. There usually is more than one way to fulfill job responsibilities. Try to accept that you and others have different work styles.

The better you understand yourself, the better you can understand others through comparison. You will also realize how to adapt to meet your needs and the needs of others by understanding the different behavioral styles. Do not let conflicts in style be a source of great stress. Develop a strategy to work with the various behavioral styles. Be other-directed when dealing with people. We will discuss behavioral styles later in this chapter. First, we want to focus on communication styles.

We usually communicate and work with others in our own preferred style or manner of working without taking into consideration the other person's style. Many times it is miscommunication that we call personality conflict. Be sensitive to the needs of others while communicating and working. How can you do this? Listen, take a step back, and observe. Accept the situation as it is, not how you want it to be. This implies that you must be flexible in your own style of working by adapting it to work more effectively with others.

Although flexibility is important, you should not do anything that is in conflict with your value system. There is a difference between *adapting* your style to work better with others and *changing* your style to interact better with others. The following descriptions offer you a method to better understand the various communication and learning styles. Be proactive in developing strategies to meet the challenges you face in each situation.

Following are two communication style inventories that overview some characteristic styles of communication. The two inventories are taken from "My BEST Communication Style" by Dr. James Brewer, and "Interpersonal Influence Inventory" by Rollin Glaser. Reflect on the various styles and descriptors. Underline words that describe your actions and write comments about the defined style that best represents you.

Another inventory, the "Orientation Inventory" (ORI), was developed by Bernard Bass. In his research on how people interact within an organization, Bass examined three variables: self, task, and interaction. The final inventory is the "Learning Style Inventory" developed by Anthony Gregorc. This inventory assesses the styles by which people learn.

By putting together a composite profile of yourself, you can identify your tendencies. Take time to reflect on why you work better with some people rather than others. The purpose of this exercise is not to categorize you or others by style, but to determine how you best interact with people and what interactions cause your stress.

These inventories help you examine your tendencies—this does not "pigeon-hole" you by saying "you are..." You are complex and ever-changing. The purpose of reviewing these various styles or characteristics is to help you identify your tendencies and to note what characteristics you may or may not show as often. These characteristics could possibly be a source of conflict or stress when you are put into an environment with others with different tendencies.

Examine and compare your characteristics with those of the people with whom you interact. Keep in mind the situation or circumstances in which you interact. Be reflective, but do not look for one "correct" answer. Develop the right questions about these characteristics—this is the key to success. When reading about the styles, underline words that you feel best describe you.

Communication Styles

Effective communication creates a mutual understanding between the presenter and listener. When you are speaking, it is essential to utilize different communication styles. You should be flexible to address the situation and be other-directed to meet the needs of the listener(s). At times, people may need long dissertations in order to grasp complex messages, but at other times a brief explanation will suffice.

Four Styles of Communication

1. Bold Style

This speaker is in charge, likes to be challenged, and tends to be brief. He or she is a poor listener and wants quick results. The positive aspect is that the speaker gives out information and responds quickly.

Thought: If you have a bold style, realize that some people may interpret you as uncaring and impersonal. Poor listening may result because of your tendency to respond or refute ideas too quickly without letting listeners finish their statements. Concentrate on what others say. You may want to take notes to be sure to collect information accurately and not respond too quickly.

2. Expressive Style

This speaker is a persuader, likes popularity, and talks too much. The positive aspect is that the speaker gives a lot of information. However, keep in mind whether or not all that information is needed.

Thought: If you are expressive when speaking, know what you want to say. Do not repeat or oversell every idea. Create a structure. Write notes or an agenda and stick to it. Do not embellish or editorialize.

3. Sympathetic Style

This speaker is sincere, likes to be a member, needs a lot of personal attention, and is turned off by aggressiveness. The positive aspect is that, by communicating with others, the speaker gives and seeks personal attention.

Thought: If you are sympathetic, remember not to be put off by others' brief styles or habit of moving quickly through information. Remember, not everyone needs the same sense of belonging or affiliation as you.

4. Technical Style

This speaker is thorough, logical, detail oriented, likes to nder, and likes low risk. The positive aspect is that the ker leaves little information out. Evaluate whether or not one has to hear it.

Thought: If you are technical, simplify what you say. At times, provide the big picture instead of great detail. Too many details often confuse the issue instead of clarifying it.

Adapted from "My BEST Communication Style," J. Brewer)

The Most Effective Communication Approach

The most effective approach to communication is to adapt your style to a balance of all four styles. This balance will help you address the various styles within a given work environment. To communicate effectively, first ask yourself what is appropriate for the situation.

Use the style of the person with whom you are speaking, then slowly move toward the points you want to make.

Bold–Get to the point
Expressive–Turn on the charm
Sympathetic–Show support
Technical–Provide details.

Listen without rebuttal. Listen to understand the other person's point of view or thoughts, then respond.

Research indicates that most people in the workplace have a tendency to use the bold style of communication. After using "My Best Communication Style" (a self-reporting inventory) with 1,182 managers, supervisors, and/or professionals (exempt) from Fortune 500 companies, the author found the following results indicating the number and percentage of people showing a preference for or tendency to use a particular style.

Bold Style–594 People (or 50%)
Sympathetic Style–262 People (or 22%)
Technical Style–205 People (or 17%)
Expressive Style–121 People (or 10%)

The point of expressing these and the following data are to have you better understand the tendencies of people in the workplace. There is no one right or best style for every situation. You will encounter all types of people. You must decide which style is appropriate for the situation. However, by reviewing all of these data, you can reflect on the style of people you work with and relate it to your style. In a small way, this information may help you better understand the work force you deal with on a day-to-day basis. Realize that even though a person shows a strong tendency in one style, that style can and does change depending on the circumstances or situation and the people with whom the communicator is interacting. Nevertheless, you can draw insight into people's tendencies.

Why do so many people use the bold style? There are various interpretations: People are direct and blunt because of perceived time pressures. They want quick results and decisions; they want to know the bottom line. They like the challenge of decisive action. At times, they might be argumentative and, when dealing with a sensitive person, they may be intimidating. The greatest flaw of this style is not being a good listener. They generally are thinking of their next statement and are not listening.

The next style, sympathetic tendency, is used by roughly half as many people as the bold style. These people are quieter and more supportive of others. They are usually effective listeners. However, they don't have the same enthusiasm, directness, or decisiveness as the bold type. They like to build relationships. These types can be intimidated by the bold types, which can be a cause for stress.

The technical style is the third most common style. These types are the detailed, structured, orderly, systematic, rational, and logical organizers. They follow the letter of the law and procedures. This style is excellent in certain job descriptions or positions; however, at times they may be expressing details to people who want general terms and the big picture or the bottom line.

The least common style is the expressive type who shares a lot of information and likes to persuade. Usually expressives relate well with other people. If they work with other types, the bold person is probably stressed by the amount of discussion, while the sympathetic-style person enjoys the rapport, and the technical-style person waits for the facts.

The various group dynamics among the styles are almost endless. Again, these data are intended to help you reflect on your style and realize why you might experience stress while communicating with these different styles.

Influence Style

Just as communication styles affect how you interact with others, they also affect the way you influence and persuade. There are four types of influence or behavioral styles.

Four Styles of Influencing

1. Assertive Behavior

This type is open, respectful of others, and stands up for basic rights. She or he communicates but does not offend.

Thought: This is the most effective of all four styles. If you are assertive, you ensure clarity of thought, and people know how and what you feel. Of course, common sense tells us that in some situations it would be appropriate to be passive or manipulative or even hostile.

2. Passive Behavior

This type practices self-denial, avoids conflict, and tries to satisfy others. This style, if it is dominant, could be a problem because the person holds so much in.

Thought: If you are passive, think in terms of expressing yourself. Write your thoughts, even if only for yourself. Express the unexpressed. Speak with a friend or discuss your ideas one-on-one with a colleague. Write your ideas before and during a meeting and read them, rather than just speaking to support what you say.

3. Concealed Aggressive Behavior (Manipulative)

This person is not open and does not consider the rights of others. This style can be harmful.

Thought: Classic examples of manipulative behavior include withholding information or responding sarcastically. At work you covet data that could affect a career decision. Generally this style does not communicate clearly and influences through nonverbals (e.g., rolling of eyes).

4. Openly Aggressive Behavior (Hostile)

This type is open but disrespectful of others' feelings and behaves in an authoritarian fashion.

Thought: You let people know exactly where they stand on issues; however, you say it in a somewhat abrasive way, ("That's stupid! Do it this way."). If you are aggressive, try to work through the disrespect. Usually aggressive people are clear communicators. However, if your style is passive or sincere, be careful not to be overwhelmed or intimidated by this style.

(Adapted from "Interpersonal Influence Inventory," Rollin Glaser)

The Most Effective Style of Interpersonal Influence

All four of these styles could be and are appropriate in a given situation. However, in a respectful and open manner, you should assert and discuss your ideas. This promotes you and your idea by building rapport and trust. Again, ask yourself why you are or are not assertive.

The following data are taken from the same group of people who took the communication style inventory. Research indicates that most people in the workplace tend to use the assertive style of behavior.

After using the "Interpersonal Influence Inventory" (a self-reporting inventory) with 1,120 participants, the author found an exceptionally strong tendency toward the assertive style. The following list indicates the number and percentage of people showing a preference for or a tendency to use a particular style.

Assertive—986 People (88%)
Passive—89 People (8%)
Openly Aggressive (Hostile)—34 People (3%)
Concealed Aggressive (Manipulative)—11 People (1%)

These results show that people in the workplace report themselves to be open communicators who are respectful or considerate of others. These data significantly show that people will speak openly as to what is on their mind and will do it respectfully. However, when the influence style data are combined with the communication style results, they indicate that people will be respectful, open, blunt, direct, and likely to assertively discuss points of view. The problem remains, however, that persons with this style do not listen effectively. They probably are thinking of their next idea rather than taking in what others are saying.

Reflect on your style. Compare yourself with the people you interact with at work or at home. Is there a combination of styles that cause stress in your life?

Identifying Your Styles

Write your thoughts about which style(s) of communication (from the "My BEST Communication Style" inventory) and which influence style(s) (from the "Interpersonal Influence" inventory) create stress for you. Which style best describes your interactive style at work?

The Orientation Inventory

The Orientation Inventory is an assessment instrument that evaluates the cause for someone to accomplish a job or responsibility. Bass has three concepts: self, interaction, and task. Each of these concepts is defined in detail on the following pages. Note that being task-oriented can be a great source of stress if the person feels pulled from a job (task) that he or she wants to accomplish.

Reflect on the three definitions and associated characteristics. Underline the words that describe your actions and write comments about the defined style that best represents you. Write notes in your book or notebook.

Description

How you react to the challenge of a job and to those working with you depends upon the kinds of satisfactions and rewards you seek, as well as dissatisfactions most disturbing to you. Basically, there are three kinds of satisfaction: getting the job done, having an enjoyable time with others, and gaining some self-satisfying ends. This three-fold classification is drawn from a theory of interpersonal behavior in organizations. As a result of years of research and development, the theory was captured in the Orientation Inventory. Remember that each of us possesses all three characteristics; however, usually one is dominant.

Three scores are obtained from this inventory:

1. *Self-orientation:* Reflects the extent to which a person expects direct rewards regardless of the job he or she is doing or what effect it has on others. For a person with this orientation, a group is "...literally a theater in which certain generalized needs can be satisfied. The other members are both the remainder of the cast as well as an audience for which the self-oriented member can air

personal difficulties, gain esteem or status, argue, or dominate." A person with a high self-orientation score is more likely to be rejected by others, to be introspective, to be dominating, and to be unresponsive to the needs of others. These persons are concerned mainly with themselves, not with coworkers' needs or the job to be done. This could also be a person who always gives to others and who is worried about what each person can do for the other.

Thought: These people are competitive, inflexible, motivated by external rewards or punishment, usually do not put others at ease, and want to know what and how well they did. This is not a negative behavior, although some people think the self-orientation is wrong. Basically it indicates, "I will get the work done but on my own terms." It is a self-perception that "work goes through me." It could result from a person who feels "I give a lot, or what is accomplished is through me. I have to do it."

2. *Interaction Orientation:* Reflects the extent of concern with maintaining happy, harmonious relationships in a superficial way, often making it difficult to contribute to the task at hand or to be helpful to others. Interest in group activities is high but not ordinarily conducive to the progress of the group in completing tasks.

   Thought: These people have a strong need for affiliation, are greatly affected by knowing that the group is succeeding or failing, and do not stay on target to get the job completed. These people will get the job done but give or need support from others. The building of relationships and social factors is very important.

3. *Task Orientation:* Reflects the extent to which a person is concerned about completing a job, solving problems, working persistently, and doing the best job possible. Despite the concern with the task, the task-oriented member tends to work hard to make the group as productive as possible. If the person is interested in what the group is doing, he or she will fight for what is right.

   Thought: These people need to complete the job and get persistent external rewards. They are driven to do better, to help members express ideas, to encourage high productivity, and to offer original ideas. Conflict can arise when someone may have another way of doing something or when they work in an environment that has a lot of interruptions (phone calls, meetings, drop-ins).

   (Adapted from B. Bass)

The author used this self-reporting Orientation Inventory with 867 participants who had completed the two inventories discussed previously. In tabulating the results, he found a strong tendency toward task orientation. The following list indicates the number and percentage of people showing a preference for a tendency to use a particular task orientation.

Task Orientation—614 People (71%)
Self-Orientation—166 People (19%)
Interaction Orientation—87 People (10%)

The results significantly indicate that these people were very task oriented. Your first response to this may be to assume that it indicates that people want to get their work done. However, stress can come into play when two people who are task oriented have differing viewpoints as to how to get the job accomplished. Self- and the interaction-oriented people often create conflict for task-oriented people because they interrupt completion of tasks, thus creating stress.

Further analysis indicates that task-oriented people do not work well with self- or interaction-oriented people. The reason was that these people would pull them off task. Task-oriented people create their stress by placing demands on themselves: "I have got to do this." If a workday is unrealistically scheduled, the task-oriented person will create great stress, which can and usually does accumulate from day-to-day. Therefore, everything is a crisis, and the environment is stressful. This is a good reason for vacations and for implementing methods for tension discharge.

Once again, reflect on your orientation and the people with whom you interact at work and at home. Write your thoughts as to which style(s) best describes you and what you can do to interact more effectively.

Learning Log for Orientation Inventory

Learning Styles

Some people are structured in their approach to learning and others are flexible. Some have a great need to accomplish, while others can discuss issues forever. The "Learning Style" inventory identifies how someone thinks about and approaches learning situations.

Take Thomas Edison as an example. Edison once had to build a crate to ship dishes. He built the crate, put in the dishes, and pushed the crate out of a second floor window to test its strength. When he invented the light bulb, he tried everything he could find as a filament. His approach was by doing, building, and testing. On the other hand, Albert Einstein discussed, theorized, and intuitively approached the world of physics. His ideas laid dormant for many years before other physicists concretely realized his ideas.

Edison was a doer who used a trial-and-error approach to getting the job done. He probably would not have worked well with Einstein who theorized and did not worry about tasks. Nevertheless, both men contributed a great deal to the world of science. There are many ways to perform or act yet reach the same objective. There is not one "right" way to do a job; usually several different approaches can be used.

On the following pages are descriptions of various learning and working styles. Identify your style or characteristics as you read the descriptions. Contemplate how conflict or stress arises among these styles because of differing mannerisms or characteristics of the people who interact with you.

There is no right or wrong way to act as a human being. However, in any situation you should ask yourself what is appropriate and what needs to be accomplished, what are the needs of others with whom I am interacting, and what are my needs and abilities. This is a way for you to realize that you may be frustrated, anxious, or distressed by people because they operate in and view the world differently than you do. We do not live in a vacuum; therefore, people need to know how best to work with others.

Learners can assume various styles based on what is available in the environment, the information presented, the level of comprehension and interest, and the desire to learn. Reflect on your own style of learning in given situations. There are four combinations as seen on the next page.

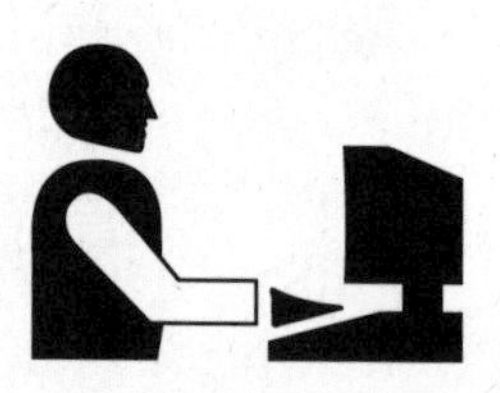

Concrete (C)

- A doer; likes hands-on experience
- Likes to experience rather than think

Abstract (A)

- A thinker; theory based
- Analytical; follows logic

Structured (S)

- An analyzer; concerned with details
- Follows a step-by-step approach
- Low tolerance for distractions

Random (R)

- A problem solver
- Flexible structure
- Likes to do different things at the same time
- Accepts feedback

Combinations

In addition to these general categories, there are four combinations. That is, the person can have tendencies toward a concrete or abstract learning style combined with a structured or random one.

Concrete Structure: needs to experience; works in a structured manner; follows orders (e.g., auto mechanic, surgeon)

Concrete Random: needs to experience; flexible; good at trial-and-error work (e.g., Edison, researcher)

Abstract Structured: thinker; structured; analytical; logical; sees the answers to problems (e.g., photographer, engineer)

Abstract Random: thinker; flexible; sees gray, not black-and-white results; sees the whole concept; people oriented (e.g., Einstein, teacher)

(Adapted from Anthony Gregorc)

To work productively with others, adapt your style to get the appropriate results. Sometimes great conflict can occur between structured and random people and concrete and abstract people. Reflect on how best to work with others.

The purpose of providing this information is to help you identify and appropriately apply your learning style. In your work situation, encourage others by learning to meet their work needs, as well as understanding and meeting your own. Realize that sometimes creative ideas are lost because they are not presented and/or learned appropriately in the work situation.

After using the Learning Styles Inventory with 1,207 participants, Gregorc found a strong tendency toward concrete random style; however, the number of persons showing a tendency toward abstract structured style is almost as great. The following list indicates the number and percentage of people showing a preference for or a tendency to use a particular learning style.

Concrete Random Style—466 People (39%)
Abstract Structured Style—404 People (33%)
Concrete Structured Style—237 People (20%)
Abstract Random Style—100 People (8%)

Analyzing the results from the Learning Style Inventory indicates a tendency for hands-on approaches and getting the job done in a flexible manner. Also prevalent is the abstract and structured style, which indicates people develop business strategies or plans and then act. The abstract structured style is the more theoretical and linear thinker.

There may be some cause for concern with opposites working together, such as concrete random and abstract structured thinkers. However, if these opposites give each other the freedom to work according to their preference, great creativity will emerge. This is known as a tight-loose relationship. The theoretical, structured thinker can establish the agenda items and possibly the process; the hands-on thinker can act on the ideas and will be flexible in applying the ideas. This, of course, is the ideal situation: Too often the higher-ranking person tries to impose his or her thinking on lower-ranking people in the organization. This is what often occurs with relationships between a parent and child, teacher and student, manager and employee, and executive and manager. One tries to impose thoughts and processes on the other. This lack of freedom to use a personal style can and does cause stress.

Reflect on your style and the style of others with whom you interact. Write your thoughts as to which style(s) best describes you and which style(s) would create stress for you.

Learning Styles Log

Summary

The purpose of presenting this information is so you will be reflective about yourself. The better you understand yourself the better you will understand others. Why? Because we all tend to compare the wants and needs of others to our own, rather than what they as individuals have to offer and how they could help and support us. When we create expectations without sharing, not effectively listening, not trusting and dealing with the present on its own terms, transferring the past problems to the present, we create unrealistic wants, needs, and desires—all causes of stress. By reviewing these different styles, tendencies, and orientations (behaviors and styles), we might better understand and be able to work with others and lessen our stress and anxiety within the workplace and at home.

There are no right or wrong styles as we view these particular characteristics or tendencies. However, there are tendencies or styles that, when used with certain people or in a particular situation or circumstance, are very inappropriate and cause stress. Why do people try to impose their way, their viewpoint, and their terms, without being open and trusting? That's a million dollar question. We all talk about being open, wanting to be accepted, but we get into situations with deadlines or multiple assignments, and we begin to impose. Often we do not even realize the stress, anxiety, and/or uncomfortable situations that we create.

It is important for you not to tell people your interpretation of their styles. However, be reflective of yourself and better understand what is occurring in a relationship that causes stress or a very comfortable feeling. Reflect on the opposites that cause stress or relaxation in your life.

Review what you wrote in all the logs and develop a flexible plan for working with these different styles of people. You will not be able to be all things to all people, nor will you be successful in every situation. No one is and that's okay. However, you may be able to improve and better understand some relationships and feel better about yourself. If you feel better about yourself, you understand the purpose of this section, and you will have successfully lessened stress and enhanced your life.

Give yourself credit for what you do or have done well. Listen and understand before you respond. Understand the other person's words, actions, and intentions and give meaning to them. The beauty of life is accepting yourself unconditionally and continuing to utilize your strengths and goodness to better understand yourself.

Summarize your comments about these four inventories. Write strategies to lessen the stress you feel based on communication, influence, orientation, and learning style.

Your Characteristics	Characteristics of Others	Continue or Adapt Your Style

Stress and the Telephone

The telephone introduces a stressor in the workplace and even at home because it is a source of constant interruption. People who are structured and task-oriented find interruptions a source of stress. Voice-mail systems offer one way to lessen the interruptions; however, many people find this device a frustrating way to communicate because they are not communicating on a personal level. Also, many people now dump information into these systems, adding to our responsibilities.

The phone is a major part of our fast-paced corporate society. All employees need to be proactive in addressing these issues. To use the phone effectively, set a time and date for callbacks, just like any other meeting. Set a time that is off the hour (i.e., 9:15 or 9:45 a.m.) to make calls, rather than at 9 a.m. or Tuesday morning. Be specific and follow up.

Questions About Using the Phone

1. Who is to answer the phone?
2. How should the phone be answered?
3. What is the timetable for returning a call?
4. What is the procedure for handling an irate caller?
5. When should a caller be put on hold?
6. How are the high-technology devices of electronic mail or phone answering systems addressed?

The most successful phone users are "attentive listeners." Do you realize that when someone calls it is generally a compliment? Many business phone calls are to acquire information or to solve problems. Usually, when you receive a call you are providing a service.

Generally, the purpose of a phone conversation is to exchange information. Actively listening to what is said, without rebuttal, then responding openly creates a clear concept of the information being exchanged. People often speak at the same time when using the phone, which is unproductive. The brain can only process words sequentially, not simultaneously. If you are speaking on the phone and the other person begins to speak, realize that no one is listening. Common sense tells you to stop speaking and listen.

When you utilize the phone effectively, you provide an opportunity for clear communication. Therefore, it is paramount that you (listener, speaker) have a clear concept of your needs. Establish the purpose (what you want to accomplish) and the importance of any action. Phone conversations are measurable if you know what you want to accomplish. This ties into the productivity effectiveness of your job quality. Make an outline before you call. Take notes during your conversation. Follow up with a memo after an important call. Specify action, dates, pricing, and so on. You should not conclude a phone conversation until you have gathered or conveyed what you want.

General Comments

1. You probably will have to repeat yourself when disseminating particular information over the phone. This is also a way in which people are influenced—they hear it, interpret, understand, and restate.
2. Paraphrasing is a must in a phone conversation. To ensure understanding, repeat what the speaker has said. Examples: "Let's go over that again...; Can we clarify that...? Did I understand you to say...? So I can...Then we will...During that time you will...I will..."

3. Always have a pencil and paper near the phone to take notes. Visual reminders will help you to organize your thoughts, recall salient points, emphasize or expand issues, and know what information still needs to be clarified.
4. Focus your energies on listening to the speaker. Try to understand on the speaker's terms, then address your own issues. When you speak, present on the listener's level. You should continually be other-directed rather than involved with your own thoughts.
5. The phone is a useful tool if it is used effectively. Before you initiate a call or take a call, prepare yourself. What do you want to accomplish? What are the expectations of the other party (parties)? Write an agenda of ideas as a support system.
6. Do not conclude the call until you have attained the results you want or have established follow-up action.
7. Remember that phone conversations are not subject to the same influencing factors as face-to-face conversation. Make sure you identify and express conflict but, more important, express agreement. Never assume agreement—state it.
8. Use vocal inflection, pauses, interjections, and clarification to achieve your expectations for the call.

The Irate Caller—A Great Source of Stress

At one time or another almost everyone has had to handle an angry caller. Here are some steps to help defuse the situation and focus on satisfactory results for you and the caller. People may become irate because they feel under attack by someone or because of the situation. Who knows what predisposition the person has before they call. Trust yourself, have confidence to act, and remain calm.

1. Inform the caller that you can appreciate that he or she is upset (honor the resistance). Begin to collect necessary information. Remember, the only way to fight emotion is with facts. To become emotional only adds fuel to the fire. The best way to disarm emotions is with data (facts).
2. Ask only specific questions:
   a. name of caller
   b. company or firm
   c. reason for the call; identify the problem(s)
   d. pertinent background

   Try to understand the caller's point of view. This in no way shows agreement, but it is empathetic.
3. Be hesitant to transfer an irate caller. That will only add to the stress of the situation.
4. Do not blame the caller for anything and do not become defensive. Remain objective: Focus on the issues, not the person. Collect all necessary information and conclude the call.
5. Establish a mutually acceptable procedure or timetable for dealing with the identified problem.
6. Thank the person for calling.

Write notes to yourself as to the kinds of phone calls you receive (e.g., customer, other departments, supervisor, friends).

____

____

____

____

____

7. What types of calls do you generally have to place?

____

____

____

____

____

Techniques for Improved Phone Conversations

Write notes in your notebook or book as to how you can improve your use of the telephone.

1. General questions: "With whom would you like to speak?"
2. Specific questions: "What specifically do you need?"
3. Paraphrase: "Let me go over that again…; Did you say that…."
4. Focus the call on specifics.
   a. Get the caller to listen. Have the person paraphrase: "Let's go over this again." Ask open-ended questions; questions that are not answered with a "yes" or "no."
   b. Be honest, sincere, and to the point.
   c. Do not end the call until you acquire the information you need.
5. Recap. Restate the necessary information.
   a. Phone number.
   b. Reason for the call.
6. Thank the person for calling.

Clarifying Your Thoughts on the Phone

1. Find out background: Examples: situation, needs, wants, desires, time restrictions, pricing, service, and product expectations.
2. Establish rapport: What strengths can you build upon within your working relationship with your phone partner? What problems need to be addressed?
3. Probe: Ask general, open-ended questions then specific questions. Don't give solutions or answers immediately. Find the trade-offs. What are the needs? Don't use statements such as "you (or I) should have" in addressing questions. Find out rather than tell.
4. Bridge: Listen, then respond. Bridge what you heard with what you know by explaining or suggesting, and address the issues the caller has expressed.

Learning Log for Improving Phone Skills

____

____

____

____

____

____

____

____

____

____

____

____

Time Management

Today's society is filled with deadlines and ultimatums. How well you function to meet those time constraints is one indicator of your success. This success may have nothing to do with intelligence, ability, or skill development (application of knowledge in a changing environment), it simply indicates how well you manage time.

Deadlines often create stress, which can greatly alter intellectual capacity and work-related abilities and skills. Nevertheless, from the day you start school you are concerned with time. The one educational concept that is practically universal is to be on time.

Performance evaluation in business picks up on the "be on time" theme. Meeting deadlines is consistently cited as a criterion for the successful businessperson. In fact, the be-on-time theme from a learning and performance point of view can and does inhibit the potential for productivity. Be-on-timers argue that there is a need to complete something by a certain time in order to do business effectively. Anthropologist Ed Hall has identified two personality types with regard to time: displaced point people and defused point people. Generally, displaced point people arrive early, while defused point people arrive five to twenty-five minutes late, yet still consider themselves to be on time. The displaced type consider the defused type rude, while the defused type considers the displaced type compulsive. Realize what personality type you are and reflect on what is promoted within your corporate culture and the types of people with whom you work.

Time is an interesting concept. Time constraints cause stomachs to churn, neck muscles to tighten, blood pressure to rise, people to argue and generally feel miserable. We have an interesting way of dealing with time—a great stressor of our lives—we try to cheat it. We get caught up in the business game of trying to beat the clock. Reflect on how you meet the time requirements of your day-to-day activities.

Time management is the effective utilization of periods of time to complete daily duties and long-term projects efficiently. This may be accomplished by establishing priorities, developing a schedule (short- or long-term), and using problem solving (developing alternatives) to deal with the changing environment to utilize available resources, motivate employees, and so on. A high-priority responsibility is that which you are willing to start immediately.

Suggestions for Time Management

1. At the start of each day, spend five to ten minutes writing a plan of action (advanced organizer). This can lessen daily stress by helping you to visualize your thoughts and develop a schedule in writing.
   a. Prioritize. What needs to be done, and when?
   b. Allow time for interruptions (phone calls, unscheduled meetings, etc.).
2. Establish priorities. Focus your energies on fulfilling responsibilities in their sequence of importance. Be flexible to meet your changing priorities.
3. As your workday progresses, write down any additional work or projects that must be completed. Review the list at the end of the day and add it to the next day's action plan. Give yourself credit for what you have accomplished.
4. Outline projects. Indicate the purpose and level of importance (i.e., urgent, important, not urgent, or unimportant) and the expected results.

Expect to accomplish:

Employees involved:

Equipment needed:

Date of completion:

Need to inform:

Need to meet with:

Possible in-house problems:

Possible customer/client problems:

Use this outline in every business meeting you have. It will focus, clarify, and establish a procedure for working during meetings.

5. Engage in problem solving to accomplish your high-priority tasks efficiently.
6. Develop a clear system for giving information and receiving feedback on your established priorities.
7. Make sure that all involved employees, supervisors, and/or managers clearly know their roles and the project time frame in accomplishing high-priority responsibilities.
8. Analyze your greatest time problems: plan for them and solve them. Following are some typical work-related time problems.
   - Interruptions—Phone calls, unexpected visitors, etc.
   - Organizational Problems—Not knowing who does what; not knowing the amount of time or number of employees needed to accomplish high-priority tasks.
   - Time on Task—Not knowing how long it will take employees or supervisor/management to accomplish high-priority tasks. Remember, time on task does not ensure quality.

- Problems Gathering Information–Not knowing how to collect, share, and disseminate data.
- Lack of Supervision–A person must first supervise himself/herself in order to meet expectations. A supervisor's responsibility is to lead, not to perform an employee's job. Therefore, if and when a supervisor is not providing direction, time toward task completion could be lost. When a supervisor performs an employee's job, that is not supervising. Common sense dictates when to perform an employee's specific job responsibility. Internal conflict can arise from an attitude of, "I can do the job better than other employees." You must know how and when to delegate.
- Emergencies/Crises–The unexpected happens (equipment failure, employee illness/absence, etc.).
- Employee Problems–Employees not fulfilling expected results, doing much more than is needed to fulfill expected results, or duplicating expected results.
- Meetings–Essential, yet time consuming. Often there is not a written agenda for a formal meeting, pertinent topics are not discussed, and the meeting is not dismissed as scheduled. (Refer to point number 4.)
- Nonessential Work–Job responsibilities that are not presently high priority, but need to be accomplished eventually.

9. Regular meetings may be essential to complete job responsibilities within a given time frame. Updates of what has been and what needs to be accomplished should be discussed. Prepare an agenda, discuss only pertinent issues, and do not extend the meeting longer than necessary.

10. Send out FYI (For Your Information) memos. Use graphics and diagrams whenever possible. Today we need to share information more than ever. Without adequate information, employees guess as to what will occur. This single action in the workplace wastes time, energy, and money. When disseminating information, use common sense. Do not share proprietary information. Information that would preclude rumors and speculation should be shared. Save time by communicating clearly. One method is to be open and realize how to shape information and action within an allotment of time.

The Power of Influence

Having people understand and adopt your ideas is a way to be influential and persuade. Influence is the interaction between and among people that causes change or support of a concept. It results in a oneness and clarification of an idea where there might have been diversity or conflict. Influence causes a union of thought—possibly a give and take—adoption or adaptation of ideas. The point is to create a mutual understanding so time is not wasted.

"Influence is a process which works chiefly in the unconscious" (Rollo May, 1989). It begins with a feeling of trust and a willingness to listen. It may not be agreement, but there must be a willingness to mentally listen, reflect, then discuss action or outcome.

Concepts of Influence

1. Influence of Ideas

This process takes times but it is time well spent. An idea is introduced by someone to a group and it is literally absorbed, discussed, chosen as an appropriate idea, then the group adopts it as its own forgetting who originally came up with the idea. For example, you may present an idea and there is no reaction. A week later at your next meeting someone else presents a very similar or identical idea and everyone thinks it is great. Timing is a factor. Time helps to create acceptance through mental digestion.

2. *Temporary Influence by Personality*

Two people talk, one person takes on the mannerisms or gestures of the other (e.g., adopting the boss' mannerisms is often done unconsciously). Influence by actions or supporting others' actions. Model and hold yourself accountable for others to adopt your behavior—take a chance and risk. Examples: everything is a crisis; this should have been done yesterday; everyone is in a hurry; everyone is relaxed, thorough, and poised; the use of slang, jargon, or dialect is imitated. Think back on the individual characteristics you analyzed. Those characteristics can be a method by which you can save time. Effectively using those characteristics will help you to clarify communication and save time.

3. *General Influence of Personality*

This is the assuming of characteristics because of the role, authority, or position one has in a corporation. A group will imitate gestures or mannerisms of the authority. For example, you know a person is from a particular department because of the way he talks, acts, or dresses. Sometimes this hinders effective use of time because the person tries to fulfill a myth about position. They are trying to impress rather than clarify.

(adapted from Rollo May)

Influence is accomplished basically through a selection process than an adoption of characteristics and ideas. We are influenced and we influence. If one person adopts or imitates the concept or goal of someone else, influence is exerted. "Since influence is a function of the individual's struggle for prestige and power, it follows that the person who has the power in a given relationship will exert influence." (Rollo

May, 1989). Think of the various games and politics that take place in the workplace that waste time. Yet many people try to beat time, which is a continual cause of stress. By understanding the politics of a company you may put less pressure on yourself to beat time; rather you may realize the process that needs to occur.

Defining Influence

What are the differences between influence and authority? An organization can give you authority to make decisions and ask employees for work productivity. Influence is an interactive process that is earned. Influencing is a process that causes others to adopt your ideas, mannerisms, or styles when you do or do not have authority over them.

A Method to Influence

There is no set order in which you should perform the actions listed below.

- Establish direction (business objectives, the desired results, outcomes, establish a structure to be followed). This goes back to the tight/loose relationship. Establishing the structure is the tight aspect, letting people take action is the loose aspect.
- Establish a plan of action and procedures, then implement that process by using influence. The action taken must be adapted and put into practical, everyday use. The action is the loose aspect.
- Develop alternatives; be flexibly structured; listen to and openly discuss ideas; share your power and support, prestige, influence, authority. Involve everyone.
- Listen effectively. Seek to understand others first, then communicate your thoughts or give answers. You will

receive fewer objections to your ideas if you listen to and find out about any objections. Ask rather than tell. Once you know what others think, you can then bridge their ideas with your ideas; now you can identify differences and commonalities. Do you realize how much time would be saved if people did not have to repeat themselves or if there was clarity in communication? Listening effectively will save time and will enhance communication; as a result, productivity will increase.

- Discuss. Clarify your understanding. Come to an agreement. Clarify what you agree on. Most often people identify and discuss conflict and fail to come to agreement. Specify agreement before you close a communication/interaction; in that way, subsequent action is productive and correct.
- Establish a safe environment in which to discuss views and to build rapport and trust. Listen and show support and help. Share your humanness. If you do not work in a safe environment, stress is going to be a constant companion. Be proactive in addressing what is and is not supporting a safe environment.
- Establish the climate (tone): environment in which people will become ready to be influenced; a willingness to accept and trust; a readiness to believe in and accept what is said and be influenced as well as influence.
- Ways to accomplish this method of influencing include the use of advanced organizers like the daily planner or an agenda to support this process. For example, let people read the agenda, you sit quietly until they have done so. Then ask questions and listen. Visual communication is better than verbal communication in creating clarity. You can read and review

written material at your own pace. When someone speaks, listen at the pace at which they present, hear the idea, and rethink what is said or think of a response. If this is the case, then why not write everything—why have meetings? Rapport, trust, acceptance—the sharing of yourself personally is better served in a face-to-face interaction. Writing agendas saves time because it clarifies ideas and provides a document that can be reviewed. The purpose of the daily planner and agenda format is to organize your thoughts and clearly convey those thoughts to yourself and others.

Daily Planner

Date ____________

Meetings

Time	__________________	Place	__________________
	__________________		__________________
Calls To	__________________	Call Backs	__________________
	__________________		__________________

Priority Responsibilities	Time Requirements	Time Constraint Problems
1. ______________	1. ______________	1. ______________
______________	______________	______________
______________	______________	______________
2. ______________	2. ______________	2. ______________
______________	______________	______________
______________	______________	______________
3. ______________	3. ______________	3. ______________
______________	______________	______________
______________	______________	______________
4. ______________	4. ______________	4. ______________
______________	______________	______________
______________	______________	______________
5. ______________	5. ______________	5. ______________
______________	______________	______________
______________	______________	______________

Meeting Agenda Sample

Title of Meeting ____________________

Date ____________________

Time Begin ____________ Time Concluded ____________

Place ____________________

People In Attendance ____________________

Purpose ____________________

Expected Results (*What is to be accomplished?*) ____________________

____

1. Topic: ____________
Time to discuss: 15 mins.
1:15–1:30 p.m. ________
Discussion led by
____
Notes taken by
____

Decision(s) ____________
____
Action(s) to be taken ____________
____
____
Time frame to accomplish ________
____
____
People involved (*responsibilities*)
____
____

2. Topic: ____________
Time to discuss: 15 mins.
1:30–1:45 p.m. ________
Discussion led by ______
____
Notes taken by
____

Decision(s) ____________
____
Action(s) to be taken ____________
____
____
Time frame to accomplish ________
____
____
People involved (*responsibilities*)
____
____

At the end of the meeting, focus on agreement and how people feel about the decisions.

Your agenda should be viewed as flexible if changes have to take place during the meeting because of an extended discussion. However, try to conclude on time and set a meeting time to discuss other issues. Ask for a group consensus (agreement) for follow-up action. Remember, not everything can be addressed in a meeting.

To Do Lists

As you think of a responsibility or a task, write it on a To Do list. Keep in mind you do much more than you see on that To Do list. The form on the next page—I Did list—should be a separate sheet to show what you have done. Give yourself credit for accomplishments and examine if you have planned and used your time wisely.

At the end of each day many people look at a To Do list and check off what they have accomplished. Instead, try creating an I Did list at the end of the day. There are many things that you do that were unplanned (e.g., phone calls, interruptions by others), yet you provided a service. Give yourself credit for the services you provide. Many people are upset at the end of the day because they did not finish or get to their To Do list. Give yourself credit and relieve the stressors of "I didn't..." or "I should have..." Compare your To Do list with your I Did list. This will give you better insight into what you need to do tomorrow and what you have accomplished today.

I Did List

1. Phone Calls	1. Service Provided	1. Outcome
______	______	______
______	______	______
______	______	______
______	______	______
______	______	______
______	______	______
______	______	______
2. Meetings	2. Service Provided	2. Outcome
______	______	______
______	______	______
______	______	______
______	______	______
______	______	______
______	______	______
3. Interruptions	3. Service Provided	3. Outcome
______	______	______
______	______	______
______	______	______
______	______	______
______	______	______
______	______	______
4. Unplanned Events	4. Service Provided	4. Outcome
______	______	______
______	______	______
______	______	______
______	______	______
______	______	______
______	______	______
______	______	______

Time Management Learning Log

Summary

What is time? In some countries time is measured by periods of lightness or darkness. Time is a method of measurement for use in scheduling events, recording activities, and determining when to take action. We can choose to honor that imposed period, set a new time period, or disregard it. All choices have consequences. Task-oriented people create great internal stress because they want to get the job done and they race the clock. Too many people go to work and play "beat the clock." Use the calendar, not the clock, to compete with accomplishments and to initiate action.

The preceding pages offered advanced organizers to help you focus and direct your daily energies. Use the Daily Planner, Meeting Agenda, and I Did Lists as a guide for prioritizing tasks and for handling interruptions and, most importantly, giving yourself credit within the workday time frame.

Advanced organizers are an effective way to focus your time and human energy. Write comments in your book or notebook as to how you can develop better time management skills and reduce the stressors in your environment.

Do not plan unrealistically. We all want to accomplish a lot and put problems behind us. Unfortunately, time and projects do not work that way. Relax so that you can best control time when you analyze and understand it rather than compete with it.

5

Developing Methods for Change

Motivation: A Method to Deal With Stress

Motivation—the set of processes that energize a person's behavior and direct it toward attaining some goal.

Motivation can be a method of effectively dealing with stress and anxiety. It is also a method of creating change in one's life to better or enhance the environment, people interactions, and concept of self.

To begin the process of self-motivation in dealing with stress, we first must identify a need. Why is there a need to deal with stressors? Remember that motivations can only be seen indirectly. Like stressors, motivation is observed in the performance that results from internalization of external and/or internal actions or perceptions. Examples: "I feel great when I get a pat on the back; lousy when I get yelled at." "Even when I do get a pat on the back I say 'Okay, thanks' and feel lousy because I should have done more or something different." Most people do not give themselves enough credit for jobs done well; however, they anguish over complaints or problems that are minor or very infrequent.

Theories of motivation may help create change and lessen stress. Four theories of motivation are presented to stimulate concepts of need and growth by Maslow, McClelland, Alderfer, and Herzberg.

When people give feedback because they want to motivate someone, they could meet with great resistance. We are our hardest critic. Often we focus on what we did wrong even when many other people tell us what we did right.

There are four possible stages that we go through when we get feedback: astonishment, anger, abandonment, and acceptance. The purpose of feedback is to feed information forward into the future. When giving feedback you should: Focus on issues, state strengths, state opportunities for development, show care and concern, and be understanding. As you reflect on all that you have written to yourself, think in terms of how you can use this information in the future. Trust yourself to act. Challenge yourself to be motivated and to grow from this experience. Also, realize that the stages that people go through after receiving feedback are normal stages.

Four A's of Feedback

1. Astonishment–"You can't mean me!" You are shocked and surprised with the feedback.
2. Anger–"You do mean me!" Angry about the feedback; you begin to attack the person who gave you the feedback or you get angry with yourself, thinking, "I should have said..." "I should have told..."
3. Abandonment–"You can't be serious!" You refuse to believe that this is true; you think to yourself, "Blow it off."
4. Acceptance–"You are serious!" Acceptance does not mean that you agree, but rather that you are willing to accept and be open to the feedback. This last step is the phase in which feedback is the most useful. Acceptance can be the stage in which you realize your own motivation or effort to achieve your goal. On the following pages are several theories that relate needs, motivation, and stress.

Four Models of Motivation

Maslow suggested a hierarchy of needs as the basis for motivation. When a need is fulfilled, you then are motivated to move on to the next needs. However, the needs may be in a state of flux because of the people you are with and the situation you find yourself in. This theory is somewhat controversial because you actually may move from one need to another in no specific hierarchical order.

The triangle showing Maslow's Hierarchy of Need is inverted from the traditional presentation. This was done to emphasize the building process and the need to grow toward becoming fully human through self-actualization. There should be an explosion toward developing self-esteem and

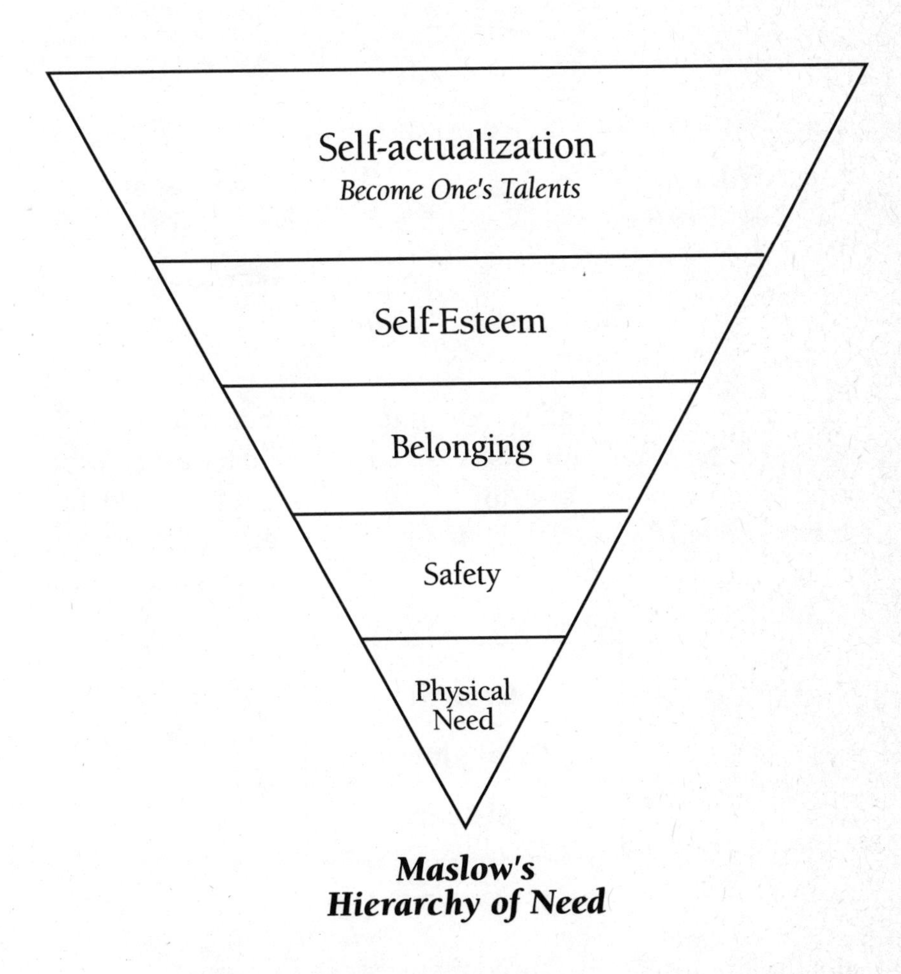

Maslow's Hierarchy of Need

talents, or self-actualizing. Where do you find your pursuit of need satisfaction on this hierarchy?

McClelland's model indicates that there are three variables to motivation: (1) a sense of wanting to be affiliated or have friends, family, or support systems; (2) a sense of achievement, a direction of accomplishment; and (3) power (personal and social), the ability to influence ourselves and others.

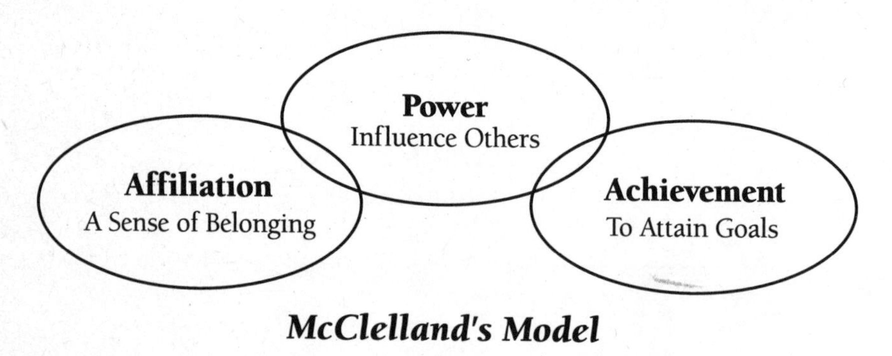

McClelland's Model

Alderfer uses different words but his concept is closely related to the other models. Existence is what we need for living, such as food and love; relatedness is the need for friends and family (social relatedness); and growth is the use of our abilities and skills to develop our capacities to develop and grow.

Growth

Relatedness

Existence

Alderfer's Model

Let's look at how these three theories are interrelated.

Achievement–Self-Esteem–Self-Actualization–Growth–Power/Influence

- All of these concepts challenge you to achieve your talents and potential and create a developmental direction. They foster a direction of growth and satisfaction.
- If these concepts are used, they will provide direction and focus for your energies (on the continuum presented earlier).
- The quest of humankind is to understand ourselves better, thereby better understanding others. Realize that you are not alone.
- We should search for whatever causes us happiness, not for happiness itself. You can find what gives you happiness through achievement, development of self-esteem, growth, power, and self-actualization.

Affiliation–Belonging–Relatedness

- These are all concepts of social interaction.
- Social interaction is a way to develop a support system for yourself.
- We all need companionship.

Physical Needs–Safety–Existence (basic, fundamental)

- Care for your body, emotionally and physically, as well as your family's needs; nourish yourself.

Any of the three models outlined on the previous pages can be a source of direction and a method to lessen stress. The more you understand how and why you act a certain way the better you will be able to focus your energies.

For instance, if you are hungry, you must nourish yourself. For the first part of our lives we do not worry about the concepts of existence or physical need and safety. We generally have someone else take care of these problems. Sometimes becoming aware of these needs is cause for great stress in young families. The sense of belonging, affiliation, and relatedness is the need to have others befriend, support, comfort, and love us. Within the concept of belonging emerges McClelland's concept of power and influence, which is a method of interacting and creating a sense of leadership and followership.

The concepts of growth and self-actualization achievement are significant as higher-order needs because the more fundamental needs must be fulfilled or met so that you can have growth, self-actualization, and achievement. Often, these higher-order needs create order and direction in our lives.

Motivation is illusive and dynamic. Motivation is seen as the effort we put out. The question is what causes you to put out effort. It is shaped by rapport, tradition, and standards (performance appraisal). An effective and useful conceptualization of motivation is one that allows us to examine, in a very real sense, the needs and levels of employees in a particular workplace; account for the needs and motivations of the company itself; and yet, on an individual basis, guide people toward self-development.

Comparing Herzberg's model of satisfiers (motivators) and dissatisfiers (hygienes) with Maslow's further indicates the difference between hygiene and motivators. One major difference that must be pointed out is that Maslow's theoretical model is built on a hierarchy while Herzberg's model has no such precondition.

Maslow	**Herzberg**
Self-actualization	*Motivatior Factors*
• creativity	• Satisfiers:
• self-realization	- Achievement
• challenges of work	- Advancement
Self-esteem	- Opportunity
• promotion	- Involvement
• praise	- Appreciation
• special benefits	- Praise
Belonging	- Earned recognition
• teamwork	- Personal growth
• social groups	- Acceptance
• friendly manager	- Work itself
Safety	*Hygiene Factors*
• job security	• Dissatisfiers:
• work standards	- Wages
• seniority	- Work conditions
Basic/Logical	- Company Policies
• money	- Organizational structure
• work breaks	- Coworkers
• equipment	- Management personalities
• work conditions	- Facilities
(Maslow, 1970)	*(Herzberg, 1966)*

The key distinction is that Herzberg's dissatisfiers offer motivation aimed at Maslow's lower needs, while the satisfiers offer motivation aimed at the higher needs. The better you understand what motivates you the better you will understand individual growth. An inability to grow can and is a cause for stress. In other words, identify a cause for your motivation and provide that level of motivation. Remember the 3 C's—commitment, control, challenge—what sense of motivation do you have?

What causes us to use our potential to grow and to experience life fully? Often, we let the direction in our lives flow haphazardly. Take charge of that direction and focus your energies toward accomplishing what you want. Take the opportunity to get and achieve what you are capable of attaining. Life has many paths. Our travels can take us over the road; our minds should give the trip a direction. There is risk in acting and in not acting. The beauty of life is that we make choices, accept our decisions, possibly alter our course, and go on.

6

In Closing

Directing Your Energies Toward Change

It is essential to identify and to focus your energies on accomplishments. You cannot react to changing situations and feel a sense of accomplishment if you have not identified your purpose and your expected results (goals, expectations). You must know what you want and how to meet your expectations.

One way to lessen a stressful situation is to identify your expectations and roadblocks. Write out your thoughts regarding the problem and develop a strategy to solve it. Remember to utilize your strengths for self-development. The act of writing your thoughts can be a method by which to lessen stress and direct your energy and implement your strengths. Instead of churning the ideas in your mind, put them on paper. You can read and analyze them; you can distribute your thoughts and get feedback. You may even change your mind about a stressor by analyzing and comparing feedback. Go back through this book or your notebook. If you completed the interactive exercise it is filled with your thoughts about direction.

Whenever you have a source of stress, write about it and/or draw a diagram representing your thoughts. Identify what will motivate you toward change. You may be surprised at your reaction to what you wrote a week ago concerning your expectations and problems. Such records offer a way to log your thoughts and to recognize seasonal problems or consistent family, employee, or self-related stressors. After you contemplate and express your ideas in writing, think of ways to create needed change.

Stress can result from the unknown—not knowing your job responsibilities, not knowing how to achieve, not knowing when tasks must be accomplished and what resources are available to you. It is essential that you become more aware of these things in order to perform your responsibilities at an acceptable level and to lessen your stress. Have the courage to continue; ask difficult questions of yourself and others.

Identify your job responsibilities by writing them down. Identify your goals along with corporate expectations. Are they realistic in regard to your workload? Your energies are in a state of flux within an ever-changing organizational environment. Be flexible and realistic; place accountability on accomplishment and self-fulfillment at an appropriate level.

Action Plan Outline

Write the actions you can take to lessen the stress in your life. Before you write, take a few minutes to reflect upon how to organize and how to implement your thoughts. Review all of your notes and fantasize about lessening stress, developing changes, and feeling good about yourself. This is a first step. Continue this process on a life-long focus of energy.

____

____

____

____

____

____

____

____

____

____

____

____

____

____

____

____

____

Signature ______________________________________

Date ________________ Evaluation Date ____________

Summary

You have taken the time to work through this book to identify causes of your stress. You may want to review this book and your notebook periodically to recapture your feelings and strategies for reducing stress in your life. You may also find that you change over time.

Today we live in pressure-filled work environments that demand a great deal from us. Give yourself credit for what you have accomplished and focus on what you have yet to achieve. Move toward the self-development of your potential and free yourself from the barrier of stress. This is not easy to do, but you can do it. The future holds many possibilities for you to explore and to direct yourself. Be reflective and don't second-guess your decisions. Choose a direction and focus your energies. Set your spirit free to fly toward your life's goals. Release air from your balloon so you are not stressed to the point of popping. Throw cool water into your boiling kettle. Learn to dissipate your stress.

Continue to revisit this book and your writings at least every three months. Use the book and your reflective writing as a benchmark. This book should be a method of assessing growth and change, tackling new stressors, and determining how effectively you have reduced stress in your life.

By trusting yourself to take action you will find a better quality of life. Care for yourself. This book is a method by which you can heal yourself.

Bibliography

Publications

Alderfer, C. *Existence, Relatedness and Growth.* New York: Free Press, 1972.

Baron, Robert A. *Behavior in Organizations.* Boston: Allyn and Bacon, Inc., 1986.

Bellach, A., and M. Hersen. *Behavioral Assessment.* New York: Pergamon Press, 1988.

Bradshaw, J.L., and N.C. Nettleton. *Human Cerebral Asymmetry.* New York: Prentice-Hall, Inc., 1988.

Dunnette, M. *Educational Handbook of Industrial and Organizational Psychology.* Chicago: Rand McNally, 1976.

Egan, G. *The Skilled Helper: A Systematic Approach to Effective Helping.* Belmont: Brooks-Cole Publishing Company, 1986.

Eitzen, D. *In Conflict and Order Understanding Society.* Boston: Allyn and Bacon, Inc., 1978.

Frankl, V.E. *Man's Search for Meaning.* New York: Pocket Books, 1959.

Frederick, P., et al. *Depression in Family Practice.* New York: Pfitzer Laboratories, 1980.

Grief, B., and P. Munter. *Tradeoffs: Executive Family and Organizational Life.* New York: New American Library, 1980.

Hall, J. *Models of Management: The Structure of Competence.* Texas: Woodstead Press, 1988.

Herzberg, F. "One More Time: How Do You Motivate Employees?" Boston: *Harvard Business Review,* 1966.

—. *Work and Nature of Man.* Cleveland World Publishing, 1966.

Holmes, T.H., and R.H. Rahe. "Social Readjustment Rating Scale." *Journal of Psychomatic Research,* 1967: 11, 213-218.

Kaplan, H., and B. Sadock. *Comprehensive Textbook of Psychiatry/IV.* Baltimore: Williams and Wilkins, 1985.

Karp, H. *Personal Power: An Unorthodox Guide to Success.* New York: American Management Association, 1985.

Lawless, D.J. *Organizational Behavior,* 2nd ed. New Jersey: Prentice-Hall, Inc., 1979.

Maslow, A. *The Farther Reaches of Human Nature.* New York: Viking Press, 1970.

—. *Motivation on Personality*, 2nd ed. New York: Harper and Row, 1970.

Matteson, M., and J. Ivancevich. "Note on Tension Discharge Rate as an Employee Health Status Predictor." *Academy of Management Journal,* 1983: 26, 540-545.

May, R. *The Art of Counseling.* New York: Gardner Press, 1989.

McClelland, D. "Achievement Motivation Can Be Developed." *Harvard Business Review:* November-December 1965.

McClelland, D., and D. Burnham. "Power Is the Great Motivator. *Harvard Business Review:* March-April 1976.

Mussen, P.H., et al. *Psychological Development: A Life-span Approach.* New York: Harper and Row, 1979.

Orstein, R. *The Psychology of Consciousness.* New York: Penguin Books, 1972.

Ostrander, S., and L. Schroeder. *Superlearning.* New York: Delacorte Press, 1979.

Porter, L., Lawler, E., and R. Hachman. *Behavior in Organizations.* New York: McGraw-Hill, 1975.

Schoenewolf, G. *101 Therapeutic Successes.* Northvale, New Jersey: Jason Aronson, Inc., 1989.

Selye, H. (Ed.). *Selye's Guide to Stress Research. Vol. 1.* New York: Van Nostrand Reinhold, 1980.

Shaw, J.B., Riskind. "Predicting Job Stress Using Data From the Position Analysis Questionnaire." *Journal of Applied Psychology,* 1983: 68, 253-261.

Skinner, B.F. *About Behaviors.* New York: Vintage, 1976.

Statt, D. *Dictionary of Psychology.* New York: Harper and Row, 1981.

Tallman, J., et al. "Receptors for the Age of Anxiety: Pharmacology of the Benzodiazepines." *Science,* January 1980: 207, 272-281.

Tobias, L. *Psychological Consulting to Management: A Clinician's Perspective.* New York: Brunner/Mazel, 1990.

Weeks, C. *More Help for Your Nerves.* New York: Bantam Books, 1987.

Videos

Bousustow, S. Productions. *Your Own Worst Enemy: Stress.* McGraw-Hill Film.

Hall, J. *Finding Time.* CRM Films.

McClelland, D. *A New Look at Motivation.* McGraw-Hill Film.

Audiotapes

Maslow, A. (1965). *Self-Actualization.* Dolphin Tapes.

Inventories

Bass, B. *Orientation Inventory.* Consulting Psychological Press Inc., 577 College Avenue, Palo Alto, California 94306 (Qualified users only)

Brewer, J. *My BEST Communication Style.* Organization Design and Development, Inc. (215) 279-2002.

Glaser, R. *Interpersonal Influence Inventory.* Organization Design and Development, Inc. (215) 279-2002.

Gregorc, A. *Gregoric Style Delineator.* Doubleday Road, Columbia, Connecticut 06237.

Jaffe, D., Orioli, E., & Cynthia, S. *Stress Map.* Essi Systems. Ashbury Street, San Francisco, California 94117.